MAMMA MIA

Italian food like Mamma used to make

Frank Bordoni

FALL
RIVER
PRESS

Project Editor: Asha Savjani
Additional text: Robert Davies
Editorial Assistants: Tanya Laughton, Camilla Barton, Carly Beckerman
Designers: Susi Martin, Chris Taylor
Art Director: Michael Charles
Managing Editor: Donna Gregory
Publisher: James Tavendale

Fall River Press
122 Fifth Avenue
New York, NY 10011

ISBN: 978-1-4351-1706-8

QTT.MMIA

Printed and bound in China

10 9 8 7 6 5 4 3 2 1

Contents

Introduction

If you want to eat well, and I mean really well, then look no farther than the tables of those who still enjoy the traditional Mediterranean style of eating in countries like Italy. This is where people have mastered the art of living to eat. Food is not simply fuel, but a pleasure, a focus around which the rhythm of each day and each season unfolds naturally, and where the art of cooking involves an emotional relationship between the food and the cook.

I still never cease to be amazed by the diversity and delicious flavors of Italian cuisine, but when you scratch the surface of this country's culinary credentials it is perhaps not difficult to see why. Italy expands over a sizeable piece of southern Europe and has many different regions, each lending itself to its own special cuisine and eating habits. In part due to the geographical boundaries of the Mediterranean Sea and the Alps, the diverse diets of Italians have remained largely unchanged throughout history. After all, how many other countries can boast of having a cookbook that dates back to the first century BC?

The biggest change to the structure of Italy and its cuisine came after the fall of the great Roman Empire, when Italy evolved into a body of individually governed states, each with its own separate and distinctive identity.

This was the period when Italian cuisine really started developing its regional diversity, with each area celebrating its own style of cooking based on the local ingredients, the geography, and the lifestyle of the people living there. This is still true today, so much so in fact that it is not unusual to hear Italians arguing over the intricacies and authenticity of a recipe even though they may be neighbors!

For many Italians, or those of Italian descent like me, the delights of dining are still about gathering around a bountiful and beautifully laid table, with the thrill of indulging in unforgettable dishes. Simple food made from the finest ingredients will always make a warm and loving gift to share. If you are a novice in the kitchen, pushed for time or suddenly invaded by the family, don't panic—think Italian. *Mamma Mia* is packed full of uncomplicated recipes and ideas, including a whole chapter on antipasti. Indeed some of the best family gatherings have involved a simple selection of these mouth-watering specialties from cheeses and cured meats to bread, fruit, salads, and vegetables, spread lavishly across a table.

Someone once said "to eat a country is to know a country," and this is never more true than with Italy. From the hills of Tuscany to the shores of Sicily, the real masters of Italian cooking are the people who inhabit this wonderful land. They have a pride and passion for their local produce, and celebrate all that is best from their region by reproducing coveted family recipes.

Recapturing the heart and soul of Italy one recipe at a time, this book is an authentic touristic culinary companion that allows you to absorb and understand a little of the history, culture, and passion of the country. It makes you want to get on the next flight out to Italy, sip Chianti by the lakes, and dig into the local specialties plate by wonderful plate; but more than that it makes you want to go into the kitchen to cook and to eat. Nothing says Italy like its food, and nothing says Italian food like *Mamma Mia*.

Italian courses

Most people, when they think of an Italian meal, think of pasta. And, while an Italian meal is much more than that, it is primarily the pasta, or at any rate the pasta "course" that sets the traditional Italian meal apart. This is because the Italians like to serve the starch elements of a meal, such as pasta, rice, or polenta, on their own. Let's make one thing abundantly clear: When it comes to food, the Italians have rules and they like to stick to them. The length of the meal and time devoted to sitting at the table, particularly in the evening, also reflects the importance that the nation places on the family and the time taken to build and maintain relations within it.

An Italian meal has always been an important and structured affair, with a traditional meal usually consisting of at least four courses. The first part of the meal, or antipasto, is considered to be the warm-up for the main meal and, literally translated, means "before the pasta". This is followed by the primo piatto, or first course, and is always the carbohydrate or starch element of the meal usually consisting of pasta, rice, or polenta. The second course or secondi will be the main meat, fish, or vegetable offering perhaps with a side dish or salad, and may include potatoes as the Italians still consider them a vegetable, not a starch. The final element is dessert or dolce. Although it is technically the last course, the Italian meal never quite ends with dessert. Italians always drink their espressos after, and never with, their dessert. And with or after the coffee, there are always digestivi—alcoholic beverages so named because they are believed to aid digestion.

These days such structured multicourse meals are no longer daily occurrences for many busy Italians. At home, they may have just one or two courses for dinner, and the order of these limited courses contains some flexibility. However, while the primo would never follow the secondo (as is obvious from the names), Italians will eat meals of antipasti followed by primo; or primo followed by antipasti; or less commonly, antipasti followed by secondo, or secondo served with antipasti on the side.

Whether you choose to eat the traditional four-course meal or take a more modern mix-and-match approach, one thing is certain: Italian food is best appreciated one dish at a time.

Antipasti

A formal meal in Italy usually begins with antipasti, a sort of "warm-up" before the real meal begins. They are, properly speaking, those delicious trifles that are made to be eaten before the pasta course. The antipasti course is designed to stimulate the appetite without filling the stomach. Usually served cold or at room temperature, a good antipasti selection will always have some combination of fresh bread, thinly sliced cured meats, marinated olives, vegetables, cheese, and seafood.

Italians savor every bite they eat and enjoy dawdling over their many courses in the company of friends. In fact, the word "companion" comes from the Latin *com pane*, or "with bread," meaning the people you sit down to eat with—literally friends defined by food!

Ciabatta

Ciabatta is an open-textured loaf, originally from Liguria. Sliced thinly and turned into a toasted sandwich, it becomes the ubiquitous panino. It is made from a sourdough starter called a biga.

∽ Ingredients ∾

For the biga:
⅛ tsp. active dry yeast
2 tbsp. warm water
⅓ cup tepid water
1 cup bread flour

For the ciabatta:
½ tsp. active dry yeast
2 tbsp. warm milk
⅔ cup tepid water
1 tbsp. olive oil
1 cup bread flour
1 cup all-purpose flour
1½ tsp. salt

Serves 4–6

1 To prepare the starter dough, or biga, combine the yeast and warm water in a small bowl and set aside for five minutes. In a medium bowl, stir the yeast mixture with tepid water and flour for three or four minutes, until smooth. Cover the bowl with plastic wrap and let sit at room temperature for 12 to 24 hours.

2 To prepare the ciabatta, combine the yeast and warm milk in a bowl. Stir and set aside for five minutes. In a large bowl or mixer combine biga, yeast mixture, tepid water, oil, and flour. Mix until the dough begins to come together. Add salt, change to a dough hook attachment, and knead dough for four minutes. Ciabatta dough is supposed to be sticky—do not add more flour!

3 Transfer dough to a lightly oiled bowl and cover with plastic wrap. Put in a warm spot to rise for two hours, or until the dough has doubled in size. Turn the risen dough on to a lightly floured board or counter. Using a sharp knife, cut the dough in half. Shape each piece into a large oblong slipper shape, about ten in. long. Cover with a damp paper towel and return to a warm spot to rise for an additional two hours, until the dough has doubled again. Put baking stone or quarry tiles on the bottom rack in an electric oven. Preheat the oven to 425°F (220°C) for one hour before baking. Lightly dust a pizza peel with flour and set the first loaf on the peel. Gently shake the ciabatta from the peel to the stone or tiles. Repeat with the second loaf. Bake for 20 minutes, until the loaves are a light golden color. Slide the pizza peel under the loaves one at a time to remove them, and put on a wire rack to cool.

Focaccia

Prep Time:
1 hour
Cooking Time:
15 mins

Focaccia, a flattish bread resembling a pizza base, has been known in one form or another since the days of the Roman Empire, and was probably introduced to Italy by the ancient Greeks or Etruscans. Today it is most famously a product of Liguria, where it is usually dressed quite simply. Try topping this recipe with anchovies, olives, and herbs, or serving it plain as a sandwich loaf.

∽ Ingredients ∽

1 tsp. sugar
2¼ tsp. active dry yeast (1 envelope)
⅓ cup warm water
2 cups type 00 or bread flour
2 tbsp. extra virgin olive oil
1 tsp. sea salt

Serves 2–4

1 Dissolve the sugar and yeast in warm water. Set aside for ten minutes. In a large bowl combine the yeast mixture with the flour. Mix until all the flour is incorporated. Change to a dough hook attachment and knead for two minutes until the dough is smooth.

2 Put the dough in a lightly oiled bowl, turning the ball over to coat it thinly with oil. Cover with a damp cloth and set aside in a warm spot for 30 to 40 minutes, until the dough has doubled in size.

3 Preheat an oven to 475°F (240°C). Put the dough on a lightly floured board and punch down once. Knead briefly, then shape the dough into a long flat rectangle with rounded corners, about 9 x 11 in. Brush olive oil over the surface and sprinkle with sea salt.

4 Put on a cookie sheet lined with parchment paper, or use a pizza peel to transfer it to a preheated baking stone in the bottom of the oven. Bake for 10–15 minutes until lightly golden.

Roast pepper and mascarpone soup

Prep Time:
1 hour

Cooking Time:
15 mins

Rich, creamy mascarpone is highly regarded in Lombardy and other parts of northern Italy. It is often used in desserts such as tiramisù, but also adds a luxurious note to risotti and pasta dishes. Here, it is blended with sweet peppers and tomatoes to make a velvety smooth soup.

∾ Ingredients ∾

6 red bell peppers
2 tbsp. olive oil
1 onion, chopped
2 garlic cloves, crushed
3 ripe tomatoes, peeled and chopped
5 cups vegetable broth
6 tbsp. mascarpone cheese
handful of fresh basil leaves,
plus extra to garnish
salt and freshly ground black pepper

1 Preheat the oven to 450°F (230°C). Arrange the peppers on a cookie sheet and cook for about 30 minutes, until they are charred. Transfer the peppers to a bowl, cover with plastic wrap, and let stand for 15 minutes, until cool enough to handle.

2 Heat the oil in a large saucepan, then cook the onion and garlic for four minutes. Add the tomatoes and broth. Boil, reduce the heat, cover, and simmer for ten minutes.

3 Peel the peppers, remove the seeds, and put the flesh in a food processor or blender with any juices. Add the mascarpone. Pour in the soup, add the basil, and process until smooth. Season with salt and pepper to taste, and serve sprinkled with fresh basil leaves.

Serves 4–6

18

Pear and blue cheese soup

Prep Time: 10 mins

Cooking Time: 20 mins

The best blue cheese to use in this soup is Gorgonzola, which has been produced in Piedmont and Lombardy since the early Middle Ages. While the cheese is being aged, metal rods are inserted to create air channels in which the distinctive blue penicillin mold grows. Its piquant saltiness combines perfectly with soft, sweet, grainy pears.

∾ Ingredients ∾

2 tbsp. sunflower oil
1 onion, chopped
4 pears, peeled, cored, and chopped
1½ cups vegetable broth
3 oz. blue cheese
4 strips prosciutto
ground black pepper

Serves 4

1 Heat the oil in a large saucepan. Add the onion and garlic, and cook gently for four minutes. Add the pears and broth and bring to a boil. Reduce the heat, cover the saucepan, and simmer for about five minutes, until the pears are tender.

2 Pour the soup into a food processor or blender, add the cheese, and process until smooth. Season to taste with pepper, and keep warm.

3 Preheat the broiler. Lay the prosciutto on a rack in a broiler pan and broil until crisp. Snip the crisp strips into bite-size pieces. Ladle the soup into serving bowls, sprinkle with prosciutto crisps and serve immediately.

Pasta and meatball soup

Italian-style meatballs containing parmesan cheese and fresh herbs are of very high quality and this is a dish treated with respect, not just a way of using up cheap cuts or leftover meat. If they are very large (up to golf ball-sized), they are called *polpette*; smaller, marble-sized meatballs are referred to as *polpettine*.

∾ Ingredients ∾

9 oz. lean minced beef

1 oz. breadcrumbs

½ onion, grated

2 garlic cloves, crushed

½ tsp. dried oregano

1 tbsp. grated parmesan cheese,
plus shavings to garnish

salt and ground black pepper

1 tbsp. olive oil

14-oz. can chopped tomatoes

2½ cups beef broth

1 tbsp. tomato paste

3½ oz. small pasta shells
or other small pasta shapes

fresh oregano leaves, to garnish

1 Mix the beef, breadcrumbs, onion, half the garlic, half the oregano, and all of the parmesan, and season well with salt and pepper. Roll the mixture into about 20 bite-sized meatballs.

2 Heat the oil in a large saucepan. Working in batches if necessary, add the meatballs and brown them all over. Transfer the meatballs to a plate when browned.

3 Add the remaining garlic to the pan and fry for a minute. Replace the meatballs and add the tomatoes, broth, tomato paste, and remaining oregano. Add salt and pepper to taste and simmer gently for about 15 minutes.

4 Add the pasta shapes and simmer for a further 8–10 minutes, until tender. Taste the soup and add more salt and pepper, if necessary, then sprinkle with parmesan and oregano.

Serves 4

Prep Time:
15 mins

Cooking Time:
30 mins

Ribollita

Ribollita is a Tuscan peasant soup that has conquered the world, and is now served (at high prices) in fashionable restaurants. The original, authentic soup is a simple mixture of leftover bread, pulses (usually cannellini beans), and cabbage. If possible, use the dark green and very flavorful cavolo nero cabbage, which is now grown widely outside Italy.

~ Ingredients ~

2 tbsp. olive oil

1 onion, finely chopped

2 garlic cloves, crushed

14-oz. can chopped tomatoes

1 tbsp. tomato paste

4 cups vegetable or chicken broth

14-oz. can flageolet beans,
drained and rinsed

8 oz. savoy cabbage or carolo nero,
shredded

salt and ground black pepper

1 oz. grated parmesan to serve

Serves 4

1 Heat the oil in a large saucepan. Add the onion and garlic, and cook gently for about four minutes. Add the tomatoes, tomato paste, broth, and beans. Stir well, then bring to a boil. Reduce the heat and simmer gently for about 20 minutes.

2 Transfer about half the beans and vegetables to a food processor and add a couple of ladlefuls of the broth. Process to a smooth purée, then stir the purée back into the soup.

3 Add the cabbage, bring back to a boil and reduce the heat. Simmer for ten minutes, until the cabbage is tender. Add the salt and pepper to taste and serve with a sprinkling of parmesan cheese.

Prep Time:
15 mins

Cooking Time:
15 mins

Minestrone

Minestrone is really the name for a group of soups, not a single recipe, all of which include diced vegetables and (usually) either pasta or rice. Different towns and regions prepare minestrone their own way, according to what is grown locally and what is in season. A delicious variation on the recipe below, well worth trying, is the minestrone genovese, into which a spoonful of basil pesto is stirred before serving.

∽ Ingredients ∾

2 tbsp. olive oil

1 onion, finely chopped

2 garlic cloves, crushed

1 carrot, quartered and sliced

1 zucchini, quartered and sliced

3½ oz. green cabbage, shredded

4 ripe tomatoes, peeled and chopped

1 tbsp. sun-dried tomato paste

3½ oz. angel's hair pasta
or vermicelli, broken into lengths

salt and ground black pepper

1 Heat the oil in a large saucepan. Add the onion and garlic, and cook gently for four minutes. Add the carrot, zucchini, cabbage, tomatoes, tomato paste, and broth. Bring to a boil, reduce the heat, cover, and simmer gently for four minutes.

2 Add the pasta and simmer for a further 2 minutes, until al dente, tender with a bit of bite but not soft. Add salt and pepper to taste, and serve.

Serves 4

Prep Time:
25 mins

Cooking Time:
30 mins

Rich porcini soup

Porcini are regarded by Italian cooks as the finest mushroom available. They have a distinctive flavor, aroma, and texture, and are gathered eagerly by mushroom-hunters in the woodlands of northern Italy. Particularly prized are the porcini from Borgotaro, near Parma. Luckily, dried porcini are of excellent quality, and can be used to make this luxurious soup.

❧ Ingredients ❧

1 oz. dried porcini

1 cup boiling water

3 tbsp. butter

1 onion, chopped

3 garlic cloves, crushed

1 tbsp. all-purpose flour

5 cups vegetable broth

1 lb. cremini mushrooms, sliced

½ cup sherry

½ cup heavy cream

1 tsp. freshly grated nutmeg

salt and ground black pepper

chopped fresh parsley, to garnish

Serves 4

1 Soak the porcini in the boiling water for 20 minutes. Melt the butter in a large saucepan. Add the onion and garlic, and cook gently for four minutes. Stir in the flour and cook for one minute. Gradually stir in the broth. Add the cremini mushrooms, porcini, and their soaking water. Bring to a boil, reduce the heat, cover, and simmer for 20 minutes.

2 Remove a ladleful of the mushrooms from the pan, then pour the rest of the soup into a food processor or blender. Process until smooth, then return the soup to the pan and stir in the sherry, cream, nutmeg, and reserved mushrooms. Add salt and pepper to taste and warm through without boiling. Serve garnished with parsley.

Prep Time:
5 mins

Cooking Time:
10 mins

Cappelletti in brodo

Cappelletti, meaning "little hats," are a meat-stuffed pasta from Modena, in the center of Italy. They are almost always served floating in a clear broth, and make the classic first course of a northern Italian Christmas meal.

～ Ingredients ～

5 cups chicken broth
4 oz. cappelletti
4 tbsp. white wine
2 tbsp. chopped fresh parsley
salt and ground black pepper
parmesan cheese shavings

Serves 4

1 Bring the broth to a boil in a large saucepan. Add the pasta and cook according to the package instructions until al dente, tender with a bit of bite but not soft.

2 Stir in the wine, parsley, and salt and pepper to taste. Ladle the soup into bowls and serve sprinkled with parmesan shavings.

Pasta e fagioli

Prep Time: 5 mins

Cooking Time: 30 mins

Soups combining pasta and beans are earthy and filling, and there are many different recipes. Soups like this one form one of the cornerstones of the *cucina povera* style of Italian food—simple, satisfying, often rustic food based on the good-quality ingredients available to poorer Italians from the countryside.

∽ Ingredients ∼

2 tbsp. olive oil

3 cloves of garlic, crushed

4 tbsp. chopped fresh parsley

2 cups elbow macaroni or tubettini

6½ cups vegetable broth

3 tbsp. vegetable purée or tomato paste

14-oz. can mixed beans, such as borlotti, kidney, or cannellini, drained

salt and freshly ground black pepper

freshly grated parmesan cheese, to serve

1 Heat the olive oil in a large saucepan, and sauté the garlic with the chopped parsley for about two minutes. Add the pasta and cook for two minutes, stirring constantly.

2 Pour in the vegetable broth, and add the vegetable purée or tomato paste. Bring to a boil, reduce the heat, then simmer for about ten minutes, stirring occasionally, until the pasta is tender.

3 Add the beans, and season with salt and freshly ground black pepper. Continue to cook for a further five minutes, then serve with a little freshly grated parmesan cheese.

Serves 4–6

Prep Time:
30 mins

Cooking Time:
15 mins

salad of baby squid

Tender baby squid prepared in this careful way are a world apart from the rubbery, overcooked rings of battered and fried calamari that—even in Italy—have become all too familiar.

～ Ingredients ～

2 lb. baby squid
juice of 1 lemon
1¼ cups olive oil
6 cloves garlic, crushed
3 green chiles, sliced and seeded
salt and freshly ground black pepper

Serves 6

1 Clean the squid and slice the bodies into rings. Bring at least four times the volume of water as you have squid to a boil. Add the lemon juice. Plunge the prepared squid into the boiling water and cook until the flesh loses its translucency. This will take no longer than one minute. Immediately remove the squid from the pan and plunge into cold water to stop the cooking process.

2 In a separate saucepan, heat the olive oil until one piece of garlic sizzles fiercely when dropped in. Add all the garlic. Cook at a high heat for 30 seconds, then remove from the heat. The garlic will continue to cook.

3 When the garlic pieces have turned mid-brown, add the sliced chiles and return the pan to the heat for a further 30 seconds. Remove the pan from the heat and allow the cooking to continue. Both garlic and chile should now be dark brown and crunchy.

4 Let the oil, garlic, and chile cool before you dress the seasoned squid with it. Serve on a bed of lettuce leaves.

Zucchini fried in light batter

The mild, delicate taste of zucchini makes them the perfect accompaniment to a rich, tomatoey main course.

Ingredients

1 lb. zucchini
1 cup plain flour
1¼ tbsp. grated parmesan
salt and freshly ground black pepper
1¼ cups vegetable oil

Serves 4

1 Slice the zucchini into batons approximately half an inch thick and two inches long, depending on the size of the individual vegetables.

2 Sift the flour with the parmesan, salt and pepper, then mix it very gradually with water, beating constantly to avoid lumps. Stop when your batter is the consistency of thick cream.

3 Heat the oil until very hot, dip the zucchini in the batter, and fry them in batches. When the batter is crisp and brown, the vegetables are ready.

4 Like all fried food, these zucchini should be served hot.

Asparagus with parmesan and eggs

Prep Time:
10 mins

Cooking Time:
20 mins

Asparagus is often paired with rich sauces and dressings, such as hollandaise sauce and melted butter, in European cooking. This simple and elegant antipasto is an Italian version of that theme, matching tender asparagus spears with softly melting eggs and cheese.

~ Ingredients ~

2 lb. fresh asparagus
salt
6 tbsp. butter
2 oz. freshly grated parmesan cheese
2 tbsp. olive oil
4 eggs

Serves 4

1 Preheat the oven to 375°F (190°C). Trim the coarse, whitish ends from the asparagus spears. Boil the asparagus in salted water for about ten minutes. If you can keep the heads above the surface of the water, then do; steamed, they have a better chance of remaining intact.

2 Grease the bottom of a flat, ovenproof dish with a third of the butter. It should be large enough to accommodate the asparagus in two layers only.

3 When the asparagus has cooked, arrange it in the dish. Sprinkle the parmesan over the top and dot with the remaining butter. Bake until the cheese and butter form a light brown crust—about ten minutes.

4 In the meantime, fry the eggs carefully. You must not break the yolks. To serve, divide the asparagus into four portions on heated plates. Slide a fried egg over each portion. The crusty, cheesy asparagus is dipped in the egg yolks and eaten without cutlery.

Prep Time:
13 hours

Cooking Time:
20 mins

Carpaccio

Thinly sliced raw beef, called carpaccio, was reputedly invented at Harry's Bar in Venice in 1950. There it is dressed with a mustard sauce, but it is equally good when prepared in this way. Do not be afraid of using anchovies with meat—the result is not a fishy taste, but a deeply savory and appetizing flavor.

～ Ingredients ～

1¼ cups olive oil

4 large cloves garlic

4 anchovy fillets

2 whole chile peppers

1 lb. fillet steak

salt and freshly ground
black pepper to taste

juice of 2 lemons

Serves 4

1 Heat the oil over a low heat until it is hot, but not hot enough to fry. Add the garlic, anchovy fillets, and chile peppers and let them stew in the oil for 20 minutes. On no account should there be any sizzling; you are not frying the ingredients, but letting their flavors soak out into the oil.

2 While the marinade is cooking, slice the beef as finely as you can. Lay the slices out on a flat dish, lightly salt them, add pepper to taste, and pour over the lemon juice. Remove the oil from the heat after 20 minutes. Let cool, then pour it over the beef.

3 Chill the dish for 12 hours. Before serving, remove the garlic and any intact pieces of anchovy. The chiles can be left, or you might choose to garnish with fresh herbs.

* It is important to use the freshest beef available for this dish. Ask your local butcher to advise you. It is necessary only to serve one or two ultra-thin slices per person, which will enable you to spend more on good-quality beef—essential for this dish.

shrimp with oil and lemon

Prep Time:
5 mins

Cooking Time:
5 mins

∽ Ingredients ∽

1 lb. small fresh shrimp
½ bulb fresh fennel, roughly chopped
1 oz. fresh parsley
juice of 2 lemons
⅔ cup olive oil
freshly ground black pepper to taste

Serves 4

1 Measure the volume of the shrimp and bring four times this amount of water to a rapid boil. Add the fennel and parsley and cook for four minutes. Drop in the shrimp and cook hard for a further two minutes, then drain. Discard the water and the vegetables.

2 Mix the lemon juice and olive oil. Use this to baste the peeled shrimp. Serve, still warm, generously sprinkled with pepper.

Prep Time:
10 mins

Chilling Time:
60 mins

Bocconcini

Bocconcini are tiny balls of mozzarella, usually sold in plastic tubs. They are widely available, but if you cannot find them locally, cut larger mozzarella balls into small chunks instead. Mozzarella made from buffalo milk is far superior to the cow's milk version—use that variety if you can find it. The addition of mint and chile makes this dish taste very like the food of southern Italy, which is often quite spicy.

∽ Ingredients ∾

9 oz. bocconcini mozzarella
¼ tsp. dried chile flakes
1 tsp. chopped mint
1½ tbsp. extra virgin olive oil

1 Drain the bocconcini and put in a bowl. Sprinkle with the chile and mint and drizzle with the oil. Toss to coat each ball well in the herbs, spices, and oil.

2 Cover and leave to marinate in the refrigerator for at least one hour. Allow the cheese to return to room temperature before serving.

Serves 4

Prep Time:
5 mins
Cooking Time:
5 mins

Bagna cauda

This boldly flavored hot anchovy dip originates from Piedmont. It is best served like fondue: On a cold night, invite friends to share a large warm bowl of it, dipping spears of raw vegetables (cauliflower, bell peppers, fennel—whatever you prefer) into the garlicky, oily dip.

∾ Ingredients ∾

⅔ cup olive oil
3 tbsp. butter
2 cloves garlic, finely chopped
8 anchovy fillets, finely chopped

1 Heat the oil and butter together until the butter melts. As soon as the butter begins to foam, add the garlic.

2 After 15 seconds or so, add the anchovy fillets and turn the heat down very low.

3 Remove the pan from the heat as soon as the fish has disintegrated. Serve warm.

Serves 4

Pesto and artichoke bruschetta

Crusty bread, rubbed with garlic, broiled, and dressed with oil, is the perfect base for all kinds of appetizer. It is possible that bruschetta originated with the olive-grower's habit of sampling newly pressed oil on a piece of toasted bread. This pesto and artichoke version is an elegant reworking of that basic idea.

∼ Ingredients ∼

2 tbsp. pesto
2 tbsp. crème fraîche
12 thin baguette slices
12 fresh basil leaves
small jar of artichoke hearts,
drained (12 pieces)
freshly ground black pepper

1 Combine the pesto and crème fraîche, then set aside.

2 Preheat the broiler and toast the bread until golden on both sides. Spread each toast with pesto mixture, top with a piece of artichoke heart and add a fresh basil leaf. Serve freshly prepared.

Makes 12

Mini meatballs

Prep Time:
10 mins

Cooking Time:
30 mins

Mini meatballs

In Italy, *polpettine* made of ground beef, pork, or veal are often poached in a soup or served over pasta, but they make perfect finger food if each one is speared with a toothpick.

~ Ingredients ~

6 oz. lean minced beef
¼ onion, grated
½ garlic clove, crushed
1 tsp. chopped fresh oregano
1 tbsp. grated parmesan cheese
1 tbsp. olive oil
8 oz. tomatoes, peeled and chopped
salt and ground black pepper

Serves 4

1 Combine the beef, onion, garlic, half the oregano, and the parmesan in a bowl. Season well and mix thoroughly. Roll the mixture into about 20 bite-sized balls.

2 Heat the oil in a large, nonstick skillet. Add the meatballs and cook, stirring them gently to brown them all over. Work in batches if necessary, removing the browned meatballs as they are ready. When all are browned, return all the meatballs to the pan.

3 Add the tomatoes and remaining oregano, season, and simmer gently for about 20 minutes, until the meatballs are cooked and tender. Serve hot or warm.

Primi Piatti

Primi piatti, or just primi, constitute the first course of an Italian meal, though they follow the antipasti. This course is the main carbohydrate or starch element of the meal and includes pasta, rice, gnocchi, and polenta. I have included pizza in this section as it is carbohydrate-based. It is important for Italians to match the shape of the pasta with the sauce, and of course there are unwritten rules to be observed! One general rule worth taking notice of is to match smooth sauces with long pasta, and sauces with big chunks of vegetables, seafood, or meat with pasta shapes, as they contain hollow parts which trap the chunks and help ensure a good balance of both in every mouthful. Remember, even though this course is the main carbohydrate part of the meal, these can still be light, summery dishes, served at room temperature like the minty crab, pear, and pasta salad as well as the more traditional classic hot dishes such as lasagne.

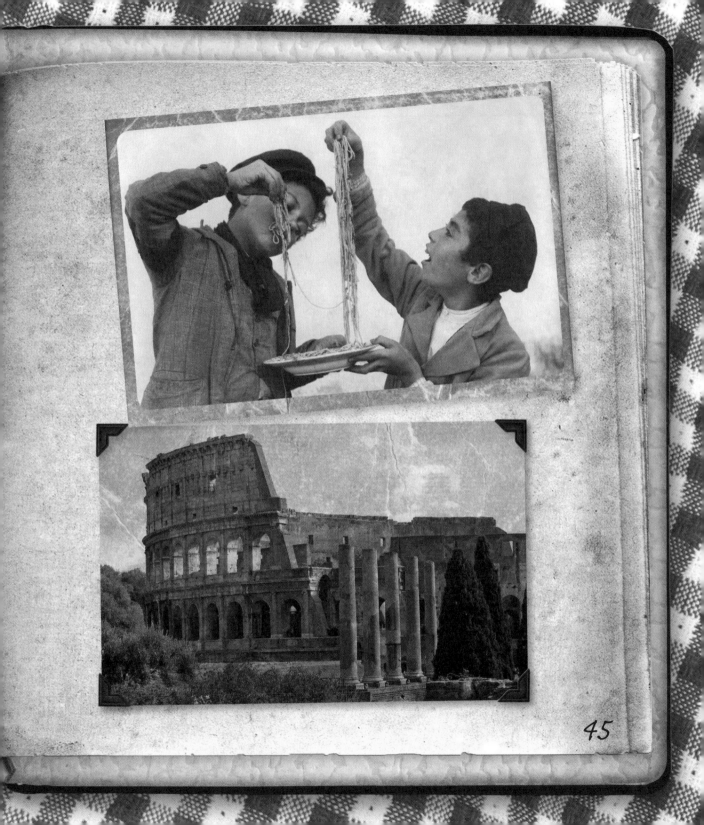

Prep Time:
45 mins
Cooking Time:
2 mins

Pasta dough

Italian families rarely make fresh pasta at home, as they can buy very good dried pasta in their local stores. But fresh pasta has a wonderful texture and flavor, and is very easy to make, so it's well worth trying out for a special occasion, just as an Italian cook would do.

∾ Ingredients ∾

3 cups type 00 flour
1 tbsp. salt
4 tbsp. sunflower oil
1 tbsp. water
3 eggs

Makes about 1 lb.

1 Combine the flour and salt in a large mixing bowl, making a well in the center. In a small bowl, combine the sunflower oil and water and beat well. Break the eggs into the well, and add the oil and water mixture gradually. Mix until the dough forms clumps.

2 Turn out onto a lightly floured surface and knead the dough for about five minutes, adding the minimum amount of extra flour to stop the dough sticking, if necessary.

3 Put the dough in a plastic bag or seal in plastic wrap and leave to rest, at room temperature, for at least 30 minutes.

4 Roll out the dough, and cut to any shape you require.

Lasagne al forno

~ Ingredients ~

12 oz. pasta dough or fresh lasagne
(page 47)
¼ cup freshly grated parmesan cheese
2 cups béchamel sauce (page 49)

For the sauce:
2 tbsp. olive oil
1 large onion, chopped
2 garlic cloves, crushed
2 celery stalks, diced
1 green pepper, seeded and diced
1 bay leaf
8 oz. lean ground beef
8 oz. lean ground pork
2 tbsp. tomato paste
2 tbsp. chopped fresh oregano or marjoram
1 large sprig fresh thyme
1 tbsp. plain flour
salt and ground black pepper
1 ½ cups robust red wine
2 x 14-oz. cans chopped tomatoes
6 oz. sliced small button or
cremini mushrooms

Serves 6–8

True Italian lasagne is not made with a sloppy meat sauce and vast quantities of béchamel. It is relatively dry and firm, and stands up on the plate rather than collapsing. In Italy, ready-made lasagne is sold in grocery stores in large tins, cut into rectangles to take away and reheat at home. But all Italians would agree that making it at home is far better, and well worth the effort.

1 Cut the rolled-out pasta into large squares (about five inches) or rectangular sheets. Lower the pieces of pasta one at a time into a large saucepan of boiling salted water. Bring back to a boil and cook for three minutes. Drain and rinse under cold water. Lay the pasta on double-thick paper towel.

2 Set the oven at 350°F (180°C). Butter a large (about 12 x 8-in.) oblong oven-proof dish.

3 Make the sauce by heating the oil in a heavy-based saucepan. Add the onion, garlic, celery, green pepper, and bay leaf. Stir well, then cover, and cook for 15 minutes.

4 Stir in the ground beef and pork and cook, stirring for 5 minutes. Add the tomato paste, oregano or marjoram, thyme, and flour. Stir well, then season well, and pour in the wine and tomatoes. Bring to a boil, stirring occasionally, then lightly mix in the mushrooms, and reduce the heat so that the sauce just simmers. Cover and cook for an hour, or until the meat is tender.

5 While the sauce is cooking, make the béchamel sauce.

6 Remove the lid, and simmer for a further 30 minutes, until the liquid has reduced slightly, and the sauce is full-flavored.

7 Ladle a little of the bolognese sauce into the dish and spread it out. Dot with a little of the béchamel sauce, then add a layer of pasta. Continue layering the meat, a little béchamel and pasta, ending with pasta. Do not include much béchamel between the layers as you need most of it to cover the top of the lasagne. Sprinkle the parmesan over the top and bake the lasagne for 45–50 minutes, until golden-brown and bubbling hot.

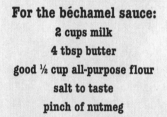

For the béchamel sauce:
2 cups milk
4 tbsp butter
good ½ cup all-purpose flour
salt to taste
pinch of nutmeg

1 Heat the milk until it is almost boiling. While it is warming, melt the butter over a low heat and stir in the flour.

2 Cook the mixture gently for two minutes over a very low flame. The mixture should not color.

3 Dribble the milk gently into the mixture, stirring as you go. When all the milk is added, bring the liquid to a boil. Keep stirring.

4 When the liquid boils, turn down the heat and simmer. Cook for a further five minutes. Add salt and nutmeg to taste.

Makes 2 cups

Minty crab, pear, and pasta salad

Prep Time: 10 mins

Cooking Time: 5 mins

This unusual combination of flavors makes for a delightfully fresh-tasting pasta salad. You could use small pasta shapes, such as penne or farfalle, instead of spaghetti if you prefer.

Ingredients

8 oz. cooked fresh pasta, such as tri-colored spaghetti

7 oz. white crab meat, flaked

2 oranges, peeled and cut into sections

2 pink grapefruit, peeled and cut into sections

2 tbsp. chopped fresh mint

2⅓ cup pecan halves

For the dressing:

2 ripe pears

½ cup walnut oil

4 tbsp. extra virgin olive oil

2 tbsp. orange or raspberry vinegar

salt and freshly ground black pepper

Serves 4

1 Put the cooked pasta in a bowl and add the flaked crab meat, orange, and grapefruit, chopped mint, and pecan halves. Toss lightly and spoon into a serving bowl.

2 For the dressing, peel and core the pears, then put in a food processor. Gradually blend the pears with the walnut oil and then the olive oil. Add the vinegar with seasoning and blend for 30 seconds or until smooth.

3 Pour over the salad, toss lightly, and serve.

spicy chicken and pasta salad

Prep Time:
20 mins

Cooking Time:
60 mins

Taking its inspiration from spices more familiar from Asian kitchens, this dish is a reminder that Italian cooking has always drawn on outside influences—even staple Italian foods such as rice came originally from the Far East.

~ Ingredients ~

8 green cardamom pods

1 tbsp. ground coriander

1 tbsp. grated gingerroot

½ onion, grated

2 garlic cloves, crushed

2 tbsp. olive oil

grated rind and juice of 1 lemon

salt and ground black pepper

3 boneless chicken breasts, skinned

8 oz. pasta spirals or twists

½ cup mayonnaise

5 oz. ricotta cheese

4 scallions, chopped

1 large ripe, but firm, mango

½ head of curly endive

1 green pepper, seeded, quartered, and cut across into very fine slices

a little chopped fresh cilantro

Serves 4

1. Preheat the oven to 400°F (200°C). Split the cardamom pods over a mortar; then carefully scrape out the tiny black seeds from the inside. Crush the seeds to a powder; then mix with the coriander, tumeric, ginger, onion and garlic. Heat the oil in a small saucepan. Add the spice paste, and cook, stirring, for five minutes. Remove the pan from the heat, and add the lemon rind and juice. Season.

2. Put the chicken in an ovenproof dish, and spread with the spice paste. Cover, and bake in the preheated oven for 30–40 minutes, until cooked through. Let cool, covered.

3. Cook the pasta in plenty of boiling salted water for about 15 minutes, or according to the instructions on the package. Drain, and rinse under cold water.

4. Mix together the mayonnaise, ricotta, and scallions. Dice the chicken, and add it to the dressing with all the cooking juices and spice paste. Mix well, and taste for seasoning. Peel the mango, and cut the flesh off the stone in large slices. Then slice these across into small pieces. Shred the endive and toss it with the green pepper; then place on a serving platter or in a large salad bowl. Mix the pasta with the chicken until thoroughly combined. Add the mango to the pasta, and mix it in very lightly; then pile the salad on the bed of shredded endive. Sprinkle with a little chopped fresh cilantro, and serve at once.

Prep Time:
10 mins

Cooking Time:
10 mins

Pasta carbonara

This classic sauce of eggs, pancetta, and cheese seems only to have been invented after the Second World War. It was popular among American troops stationed in Italy, who took the recipe back home and popularized it in the English-speaking world.

∾ Ingredients ∾

4 tbsp. butter

6 oz. panchetta, shredded

8 eggs

salt and black pepper

½ cup single cream

1 lb. spaghetti

plenty of chopped, fresh parsley

freshly grated parmesan cheese, to serve

Serves 4

1 Melt the butter in a large, heavy-based or nonstick saucepan. Add the panchetta and cook for two minutes. Beat the eggs with seasoning and add the cream. Reduce the heat under the pan, if necessary, then pour in the eggs and cook them gently, stirring all the time until they are creamy. Do not cook the eggs until they set and scramble and do not increase the heat to speed up the process or the carbonara will be spoilt.

2 The pasta should be added to the boiling water at the same time as the eggs are added to the pan. This way, the pasta will be drained and hot, ready to be tipped into the eggs. When the eggs are half set, add the pasta, mix well until the eggs are creamy, and serve at once, sprinkled with parsley. Offer parmesan cheese with the pasta carbonara.

Beef and mushroom cannelloni

Prep Time: 45 mins

Cooking Time: 25 mins

⌇ Ingredients ⌇

1 cup milk
½ small onion, peeled
small piece carrot, peeled
1 celery stalk, trimmed
2–3 whole cloves
few black peppercorns
2 bay leaves
few parsely stalks
2 tbsp. butter
2 tbsp. plain flour
salt
½ oz. dried porcini, soaked in warm water for 20 minutes
8 oz. lean ground beef
1 onion, peeled and finely chopped
2 garlic cloves, crushed
2 oz. finely chopped chanterelle mushrooms
½ cup red wine
2 tbsp. tomato paste
ground black pepper
12 fresh lasagne sheets
2 oz. mozzarella cheese, sliced

The combination of dried porcini and fresh mushrooms lends this dish an autumnal aroma and deep-toned mushroomy flavor, but you could use regular cultivated mushrooms if you prefer.

1. Preheat the oven to 375°F (190°C), ten minutes before baking the cannelloni. Pour the milk into a small saucepan and add the onions, carrot, celery, cloves, peppercorns, bay leaves, and parsley stalks. Slowly bring the sauce to just below boiling point then remove from the heat, cover, and leave to infuse for at least 15 minutes. Strain, reserving the milk.

2. Melt the butter in a small pan and stir in the flour. Cook over a gentle heat for two minutes, then draw off the heat and gradually stir in the reserved milk. Return pan to the heat and cook, stirring until smooth, thick, and glossy. Season with the salt. Cover with a sheet of dampened parchment paper and reserve.

3. Soak the porcini in warm water for 20 minutes. Drain, reserving the liquor, and chop the porcini. Sauté the beef in a skillet until browned, stirring frequently to help break up any lumps. Add the onion, garlic, porcini, and chanterelles, and continue to sauté for five minutes or until the onion is softened.

Serves 4

4 Pour in the wine, bring to a boil, and simmer for five minutes. Blend the tomato paste with the reserved porcini soaking water and two tablespoons of water. Stir into the beef mixture with black pepper to taste. Cook for 5 more minutes. Remove from the heat and cool.

5 Bring a large pan of water to a boil, add a tablespoon of salt, then drop in four large lasagne sheets, one at a time. Cook for 2–3 minutes, ensuring that they do not stick together. Drain, lay them on clean dishcloths, and pat dry. Repeat with the remaining lasagne sheets.

6 Use the prepared beef mixture to fill the pasta sheets and roll up. Arrange over the base of an ovenproof dish. Top with the prepared sauce and dot with the cheese slices. Bake the cannelloni in the oven for 25 minutes or until golden and bubbling. Serve immediately.

Prep Time:
10 mins
Cooking Time:
15 mins

Pasta salad with fresh dates

The use of dates in Italian cookery reflects the influence of Arabs on Sicilian and southern Italian culture in the Middle Ages. In this salad, the sweet fruit and peppery watercress are combined with pasta to stunning effect.

∽ Ingredients ∽

2 cups pasta shapes (such as porcini-flavored mushroom shapes, penne, or rigatoni)

salt and ground black pepper

4 celery stalks, sliced

¼ cup pine nuts

2⅔ cups roughly chopped walnuts or pecan nuts

8 oz. fresh dates, pitted and sliced

1 bunch of watercress, leaves only

4 tbsp. chopped fresh parsley

1 tbsp. chopped fresh mint

handful of fresh basil leaves, shredded

3 tbsp. balsamic vinegar

1 garlic clove, crushed

1 tbsp. walnut oil

½ cup olive oil

1 Cook the pasta in boiling salted water for about 15 minutes, or according to the instructions on the package, until tender.

2 Blanch the celery in boiling salted water for one minute; then drain well.

3 Dry-roast the pine nuts in a small, heavy-based saucepan over a low to medium heat, and shake it often or stir, so that they have browned lightly and evenly.

4 Mix the walnuts or pecans, pine nuts, dates, watercress, parsley, mint, and basil in a large bowl.

5 Whisk the balsamic vinegar, garlic, and salt and pepper to taste in a bowl; then slowly whisk in the walnut and olive oils. Pour the dressing over the nut and date mixture.

6 Drain the cooked pasta, and add it to the bowl; toss well, and cover until cooled before serving.

Serves 4

Fusilli with wild mushrooms

Prep Time:
15 mins

Cooking Time:
10 mins

Garlic and thyme are often paired with mushrooms in classic homestyle Italian cooking. In this recipe they add interest to the mixture of wild fungi, which makes up most of the pasta sauce.

∾ Ingredients ∾

3½ cups dried fusilli
¼ cup olive oil, plus extra for cooking pasta
1 clove of garlic, crushed
2 tbsp. chopped, fresh thyme
generous ¼ lb. shitake mushrooms, sliced
generous ¼ lb. oyster mushrooms
½ oz. dried ceps, soaked,
drained, and sliced
salt and freshly ground black pepper
freshly grated parmesan cheese, to serve

Serves 4

1 Bring a large saucepan of water to a boil, and add the fusilli with a dash of olive oil. Cook for about ten minutes, stirring occasionally, until tender. Drain and set aside, covered.

2 Heat the olive oil in a large skillet, and add the garlic and fresh thyme. Cook for two minutes, then stir in all the mushrooms and season to taste with salt and freshly ground black pepper.

3 Fry the mushrom mixture over high heat for 3–4 minutes to brown slightly, then turn the mixture into the saucepan containing the fusilli. Toss together briefly, then serve with a little freshly grated parmesan cheese.

spinach and mushroom lasagne

Prep Time: 25 mins

Cooking Time: 40 mins

Vegetarian alternatives to the classic meat-based lasagne al forno are common in Italy today. The trick when making this version is to drain the spinach thoroughly so that the lasagne does not become watery.

～ Ingredients ～

butter, for greasing
½ lb. fresh lasagne sheets
½ quantity béchamel sauce (page 49)
⅔ cup freshly grated parmesan cheese

For the filling:

2 tbsp. olive oil
2 cloves garlic, crushed
1 onion, chopped
½ lb. mushrooms, sliced
1½ lb. frozen spinach, thawed and well drained
good pinch of freshly grated nutmeg
1 lb. cream cheese
salt and freshly ground black pepper

1 Make the filling first. Heat the olive oil in a large skillet and sauté the garlic and onion for about three minutes. Add the mushrooms and continue to cook for about 5 minutes, stirring occasionally. Add the spinach and nutmeg and cook for about five minutes, then stir in the cream cheese and season with salt and freshly ground black pepper. Cook for 3–4 minutes, until the cheese has melted and blended with the spinach mixture. Preheat the oven to 400°F (200°C).

2 To assemble the lasagne, butter a lasagne dish and put a layer of lasagne sheets on the bottom. Spoon some of the spinach mixture evenly over it, then add another layer of lasagne. Continue layering the pasta and spinach mixture alternately until both are used up, then pour the béchamel sauce evenly over the top.

3 Sprinkle the parmesan cheese over the lasagne and bake for about 40 minutes, until golden and bubbling.

Serves 6

Stuffed Lumache

∾ Ingredients ∾

For the lumache:

2 tbsp. butter

1 onion, finely chppped

4 oz. finely chopped mushrooms

1¼ cups breadcrumbs

salt and ground black pepper

1 tbsp. chopped fresh oregano

4 oz. ricotta

1 bunch of watercress, leaves only, finely chopped

freshly grated nutmeg

16 large lumache

½ quantity béchamel sauce (page 49)

4 tbsp. freshly grated parmesan cheese

For the vegetable base:

2 tbsp. olive oil

1 large onion, halved and thinly sliced

1 garlic clove, minced

1 green pepper, seeded, halved, and thinly sliced

1 red pepper, seeded, halved, and thinly sliced

2 medium zucchini, thinly sliced

6 tomatoes, peeled, seeded, and quartered

Lumache—meaning snails—are very large hollow pasta shapes, designed to be stuffed and baked. In this recipe they are nestled on a bed of vegetables before being browned in the oven.

1 First, prepare the stuffing for the lumache. Melt the butter in a saucepan. Add the onion, and cook, stirring, for 5 minutes. Then add the mushrooms, and continue to cook, stirring occasionally, for a further ten minutes. Mix in the breadcrumbs, salt and pepper to taste, and oregano. Then add the ricotta cheese and watercress. Season with a little grated nutmeg to taste, and set aside.

2 Preheat the oven to 400°F (200°C).

3 Cook the lumache in plenty of boiling salted water for about 12 minutes, or until tender. Drain well, rinse under cold water, and drain again so they do not close up.

4 Meanwhile, prepare the béchamel sauce (page 49) and set aside.

5 Next, prepare the vegetable base. Heat the oil in a skillet. Add the onion, garlic, and peppers. Cook, stirring, for 15 minutes, or until the onion has softened. Stir in the zucchini, and cook for two minutes; then add the tomatoes, with salt and pepper to taste. Cook for 2–3 minutes, to soften the tomatoes; then spoon the mixture into an ovenproof dish or four individual dishes.

Serves 4

6 Fill the lumache with the mushroom mixture and arrange them on the vegetable base. Spoon a little béchamel sauce over the top of each stuffed lumache, and sprinkle with a little parmesan. Bake for about 15 minutes, or until the tops have browned.

Pasta with eggs and tarragon

Prep Time:
5 mins

Cooking Time:
10 mins

Tarragon is a herb especially beloved by French cooks, but it is also used to great effect in some Italian dishes. Its fresh, aniseed flavor is welcome here as it cuts through the richness of the eggs.

∿ Ingredients ∿

3 oz. butter (or use olive oil or a mixture of butter and olive oil if preferred)
3 tbsp. chopped fresh tarragon
8 eggs
1 lb. pasta (tagliatelle or penne)
freshly ground black pepper
freshly grated parmesan cheese, to serve
fresh baby spinach leaves (optional, to serve)

Serves 4

1 Warm four plates or bowls. Melt the butter (or heat the oil with the butter if used) and add the tarragon, then set aside over a very low heat.

2 Meanwhile, cook the pasta according to the package instructions. When the pasta is half done, boil the water for steaming the spinach (optional). When the pasta is ready for draining, poach the eggs and put the spinach leaves on to steam for two minutes.

3 Divide the pasta between the plates or bowls. Put a couple of eggs on each portion, then spoon the butter and tarragon over the top. Season with pepper and serve immediately on top of the steamed spinach (optional), sprinkled with grated parmesan cheese.

Pepper and pasta ratatouille

Prep Time: 15 mins

Cooking Time: 40 mins

Ratatouille is a French word we have adopted into English, but vegetable stews like this one, here served with pasta, are eaten very regularly in Italy. You might come across a similar vegetable dish called peperonata, made with peppers and onions, or—especially in Sicily—caponata, which also contains zucchini and fennel.

∾ Ingredients ∾

1 lb. pasta shells

dash of olive oil, plus 3 tbsp.

2 garlic cloves, crushed

1 onion, chopped

2 bell peppers, seeded and sliced

2 eggplants, chopped into chunks

14-oz. can chopped tomatoes

2 heaped tbsp. tomato paste

½ cup dry red wine

2 tbsp. fresh oregano

salt and pepper

fresh oregano sprigs, to garnish

1 Bring a large saucepan of water to a boil, and add the pasta with a dash of olive oil. Cook for about ten minutes, stirring occasionally, until tender. Drain and set aside.

2 Heat the remaining olive oil in a large saucepan and sauté the garlic and onion for about three minutes, until softened. Stir in the pepper and eggplant. Cover and cook for about five minutes, or until the pepper and eggplant have softened slightly.

3 Stir the remaining ingredients, except the oregano sprigs, into the pepper mixture and bring to simmering point. Reduce the heat, cover, and cook for about 10 minutes, then stir in the pasta. Cook for a further 5 minutes, stirring occasionally. Serve garnished with fresh oregano sprigs.

Serves 4–6

Chicken cacciatore

This dish (the hunter's chicken) is a very traditional way of preparing chicken, which relies on really ripe tomatoes with a good flavor, not the watery kind that are available in the depths of winter. Simply delicious served on a bed of spaghetti.

~ Ingredients ~

4 chicken joints, skinned, approx. 7 oz. each

¼ cup plain flour, seasoned

3 tbsp. vegetable oil

8 pickling onions or shallots, peeled

1 clove garlic, finely chopped

4 oz. button mushrooms, halved

1 sweet green pepper, deseeded, and cut into strips

¾ pt. chopped tomatoes and juices (canned)

½ cup dry white wine

2 tbsp. tomato paste

2 tbsp. red wine vinegar

1 tsp. chopped fresh basil

1 tsp. chopped fresh oregano (or marjoram)

salt and freshly ground black pepper

1 lb. spaghetti

2 oz. black olives

chopped basil or parsley to garnish

1 Skin the chicken joints and dust them with the seasoned flour. Heat the oil in a large pan and sauté the chicken until golden brown.

2 Add the onions and garlic and cook for a further four minutes. Sprinkle in any remaining flour, the mushrooms, and the green pepper, and gradually blend in the tomatoes and juice. Stir in the remaining ingredients apart from the olives. Check seasoning.

3 Cover and simmer for 20–30 minutes or until chicken is tender. Ten minutes before the end, cook the spaghetti and stir the olives into the sauce.

4 Serve garnished with freshly chopped basil or parsley.

Serves 4

Pasta with seafood sauce

You could vary your selection of seafood according to what's in season and available when you make this dish. Squid rings, clams, mussels, and shrimp are the most obvious choices and the ones that would be most readily at hand in Italy.

∽ Ingredients ∽

1 lb. fresh mussels

1 lb. fresh cockles or small clams (optional)

1½ cups water

2 tbsp. olive oil

1 garlic clove, crushed

1 onion, chopped

2 celery stalks, thinly sliced

1 carrot, diced

4 oz. sliced mushrooms

¼ cup plain flour

1 cup light red wine

1 tbsp. tomato paste

salt and ground black pepper

4 squid sacs, sliced

1 lb. white fish fillet, skinned, and cut into chunks

8–12 uncooked jumbo shrimp

8 fresh scallops, shelled and sliced

1 Clean the mussels and cockles or clams (if using) by thoroughly scrubbing the shells and scraping off any barnacles. Discard any open or broken shells that do not close when tapped sharply. Leave to stand in cold water overnight in a large bucket of cold water with a handful of oatmeal added, leaving the bucket in a cold place. Drain and rinse the shellfish, and remove the "beards" from the mussels–the group of fine, black hairs that protrude from the shells. Pull them away sharply.

2 Put the mussels and cockles in a large saucepan, and pour in the water. Bring the water to a boil, then reduce the heat so that the water simmers, and cover the pan. Cook, shaking the pan ocasionally, for about ten minutes, or until all the shells have opened. Make sure you have discarded any opened uncooked shellfish that do not shut when tapped and discard any shells that do not open during cooking (these shellfish are dead and may contain toxins). Reserve a few mussels in their shells for garnishing, if you like, then remove the other mussels and cockles or clams from their shells and set aside.

Serves 4

3 Strain the cooking liquid through muslin, and boil it to reduce it to about 1 cup, if necessary. Set this aside.

4 Heat the olive oil in a saucepan. Add the garlic, onion, celery and carrot. Stir well, cover the pan, and cook gently for 20 minutes, shaking the pan occasionally, until the vegetables are tender, but not browned.

5 Add the mushrooms and stir in the flour. Slowly pour in the strained cooking liquor and wine. Bring to a boil, stirring, and add the tomato paste. Stir in the salt and freshly ground black pepper to taste. Add the squid to the sauce, cover, and simmer gently for 15 minutes.

6 Then add the white fish and shrimp, and continue to cook, covered, for five minutes. Add the scallops, and poach gently for five minutes. Lastly, add the cooked mussels and cockles or clams. Heat for a few minutes without simmering or boiling. Taste for seasoning, and serve with freshly cooked pasta of your choice. Garnish with the reserved mussels in their shells.

Prep Time:
10 mins

Cooking Time:
20 mins

Fettuccine

Fettuccine is especially popular in Rome; elsewhere in Italy, people might be inclined to use tagliatelle for this dish, and to tone down the garlic. You could do likewise—and feel free to substitute any long pasta ribbons.

∽ Ingredients ∽

1 lb. dried fettuccine

dash of olive oil

2 tbsp. butter

3 garlic cloves, crushed

1 lb. frozen chopped spinach, thawed and well drained

1 cup single cream

salt and pepper

⅓ cup freshly grated parmesan cheese, plus extra to serve

Serves 4–6

1 Bring a large saucepan of water to a boil, and add the fettuccine with a dash of olive oil. Cook for about 8 minutes, stirring occasionally, until tender. Drain and set aside, covered, to keep warm.

2 Melt the butter in a large skillet and sauté the garlic for two minutes, then add the spinach. Cook over medium heat for about five minutes, stirring frequently, until the moisture has evaporated.

3 Add the cream and season with salt and pepper. Toss in the fettuccine and parmesan cheese, stir, and cook for a final minute. Serve with extra parmesan.

Basic pizza dough

Prep Time:
3 hours

Cooking Time:
10 mins

Store-bought pizza bases bear no relation to the real thing. It is surprisingly easy to make a proper, elastic yeast dough, and you will be delighted with the pizza it makes. Specialty shops and some supermarkets sell the very finely milled Italian 00 flour, but regular all-purpose flour makes a good substitute.

⤳ Ingredients ⤳

1 cup 00 flour

1 ⅓ cups all-purpose flour

¾ cups plus 1 tbsp. warm water

1 tsp. traditional active dry yeast

½ tsp. honey

1½ tsp. olive oil

¾ tsp. salt

Makes 1 large rectangular pizza crust or two 9-in. crusts.

1 To prepare the dough, combine the flour. Put warm water, yeast, honey, and olive oil in a bowl or standing mixer. Add ⅓ cup flour and mix on low speed or whisk by hand until smooth. Cover with a clean paper towel and let sit for 20 minutes, until the mixture is foamy on top. Add the remaining flour and salt and mix with a dough hook for 4 minutes, or knead by hand for ten minutes, until all the flour is mixed in and the dough is smooth. Cover with a clean paper towel and put in a warm spot to rise for 1½ hours, or until the dough has almost doubled in size.

2 If making one pizza, lightly oil a rectangular baking pan. Put the dough in the pan, and punch down once in the center. Using your hands, stretch out the dough from the center to the sides, taking care to distribute it evenly around the pan. Using toothpicks or small lightweight containers as supports in each corner, tent the dough with paper towels and return to a warm spot for another 45 minutes.

3 If making two pizze, lightly oil two 9-in. round cake pans. Using your hands or a rolling pin, stretch out each ball to form a 9-in. disc. With your fingers, work a little extra dough to the edges to form the crust. Put the dough in pans, cover with a clean paper towel, and return to a warm spot for 45 minutes.

Pizza margherita

This pizza was invented in 1889 and named after Margaret of Savoy, the second queen of a unified Italy. Its three colors—green basil, red tomatoes, and white cheese—represent the three stripes of the Italian flag.

∿ Ingredients ∿

1 basic pan pizza crust (page 73)

For the sauce:
3 tbsp. olive oil
1 garlic clove, minced
28-oz. can whole tomatoes
½ tsp. salt
½ tsp. dried oregano or 1 tbsp. chopped fresh oregano
pinch of crushed red pepper flakes

For the topping:
4 oz. baby bocconcini, thinly sliced (or sliced mozzarella)
4 large basil leaves, roughly torn

Serves 6–8

1 Make two round pizza crusts (page 73).

2 Preheat the oven to maximum setting, up to 550°F (300°C).

3 Make the sauce by heating the oil in a large, heavy skillet. Add the garlic and cook for two minutes. Add tomatoes and break them up into small chunks with a wooden spoon. Simmer for 15–20 minutes, until most of the liquid has evaporated and the sauce has thickened. Add salt, oregano, and red pepper flakes to taste.

4 Divide the sauce (approximately 1⅔ cups in total) between the two pans and spread evenly, leaving ½-in. border around the edge.

5 Distribute cheese slices around the two pizze. Bake for 8–10 minutes on a rack in the lower half of the oven, until the cheese is melted and the crust is golden brown. Sprinkle pieces of basil over the pizze. Slice into wedges and serve.

Chèvre, arugula, and pear pizza

Prep Time: 3 hours

Cooking Time: 5 mins

Arugula is cultivated in the Veneto region, the hinterland of Venice, and crops up regularly in salads and other dishes there. Here it is served as a modern, refreshing pizza topping, matched with soft, sweet pears.

∾ Ingredients ∾

1 recipe basic pizza crust (page 73)
12 oz. chèvre
¼ cup crème fraîche
3 firm, ripe pears
peeled, cored, and sliced
2 tsp. lemon juice
½ lb. baby arugula, cleaned, dried, and stemmed

Makes three 12-in. pizze

1 Preheat oven to maximum setting, up to 500°F (250°C). Put pizza stone or unglazed tiles on the bottom of a gas oven or the lowest rack of an electric oven.

2 Following the instructions on page 73, make three 12-in. discs of pizza dough. Lightly dust a pizza peel with flour or cornmeal and put one disc of pizza dough on the peel.

3 In a bowl, combine chèvre and crème fraîche until smooth. Toss the pear slices in lemon juice to prevent discoloration. Spread a third of the chèvre mixture over the crust, leaving a half-inch border around the edge. Arrange slices from one pear over the chèvre mixture. Put half a cup baby arugula leaves over the pear slices. Gently shake the pizza from the peel to the stone or tiles.

4 Bake for four to five minutes. Repeat with the remaining two pizze.

Prep Time:
40 mins

Cooking Time:
30 mins

Calzone

Calzone—a kind of folded pizza, stuffed with tomatoes, ham, and cheese—makes a perfect portable lunch, and in Italy they are often sold by street vendors or in small takeout stores to be eaten while you stroll around a town or market.

∽ Ingredients ∼

5 cups plain flour

1 tbsp. caster sugar

1 tbsp. instant-rise yeast

1 tsp. salt

1½ tsp. extra-virgin olive oil

1 cup very warm water

7 oz. ricotta cheese

3 oz. mozzarella cheese cut into ¼-in. cubes

2 tbsp. grated parmesan cheese

3 oz. prosciutto, roughly chopped

2 tbsp. finely chopped fresh basil

freshly ground black pepper

Makes 4

1 Preheat the oven to maximum setting, up to 450°F (230°C). To prepare the pizza dough, combine ten ounces of the flour with the sugar, yeast, and salt. Set aside. Warm the olive oil and water in a small saucepan over low heat. Slowly stir in the water and oil into the flour mixture until well combined. Stir in five ounces flour. Add up to 2½ oz. more flour as necessary to make a firm dough. Turn onto a lighly floured surface and knead until the dough is smooth and elastic (about ten minutes). Lightly grease a large bowl with olive oil.

2 Put the dough in the bowl and cover with a clean paper towel. Set aside for ten minutes. While the pizza dough is sitting, prepare the filling. In a large bowl, combine the cheeses, prosciutto, and basil. Add freshly ground black pepper to taste. When the dough has rested for ten minutes, punch it down. Cut the dough into four pieces, shaping each ball and flattening to form a disc. Lightly flour each disc. On a lightly floured surface, roll out each disc ⅛-in thick and 6 in. round. Add flour as necessary to prevent sticking. Using a pastry brush, glaze the top edge of the circles with water. Spoon a quarter of the filling onto the lower half of each circle. Fold the top over and press the edges to seal. Crimp decoratively and make two slits in the top. Put the calzoni on a baking sheet lined with parchment paper and bake on the middle rack for 30 minutes, or until the filling is hot and the crust is golden brown.

Pancetta and mortadella pizza

Prep Time:
3 hours

Cooking Time:
45 mins

This *pizza rustica* (pizza pie) features a spectacular blend of smoked cheeses and cured meats. Mortadella is the product adapted by American cooks to make bologna sausage, which lacks the distinctive pearls of white fat found in mortadella; the original Italian sausage should be used in this recipe.

∽ Ingredients ∽

1 recipe basic pizza dough
(page 73)
1-2 mild Italian sausages, removed
from casings
¼ lb. pancetta, cubed
1 tbsp. extra virgin olive oil
¼ lb. mortadella, cut into small pieces
1 cup ricotta cheese
¼ cup smoked provolone cubes
½ cup shredded mozzarella
¼ cup finely grated parmesan
2 eggs, lightly beaten
1 garlic clove, minced
2 tbsp. chopped flat-leaf parsley
pinch crushed red pepper flakes
freshly ground black pepper

1 Preheat the oven to maximum setting, up to 400°F (200°C). While the dough is in its second rising, make the filling. Fry the crumbled sausage meat and pancetta cubes in olive oil for five to 6 minutes, until the sausage is cooked through (remove the pancetta from the pan earlier as it gets crispy).

2 Drain and put in a large bowl. Add mortadella, cheeses, eggs, garlic, and seasonings, and stir until well combined.

3 On a lightly floured surface, roll out the first ball of dough to a 12-in. round. Add flour as necessary to prevent sticking. Put the dough in a 9-in. springform pan, so there is an inch hanging over the edge.

4 Pour the filling into a pan. Roll out a second ball to a 9-in. round and put over the filling. Fold the overhanging dough from the bottom crust over the edge of the top crust, pinching lightly to seal. Make two slits in the top to allow steam to escape.

5 Bake in the middle of the oven for 45 minutes. Let sit for 10–15 minutes before slicing into eight wedges.

Serves 8

Sausage and mushroom calzoni

The basic calzone filling of ham, cheese, and tomatoes remains the most familiar version, but Italian cooks do experiment with other fillings. Here is my favorite; it's especially good if you use a good-quality sausage with a high proportion (90%) of pork.

~ Ingredients ~

1½ cups all-purpose flour

1½ cups bread flour

1 tsp. granulated sugar

2 tsp. quick-rise yeast

1 tsp. salt

1½ tbsp. extra-virgin olive oil

1 cup warm water

12 oz. Italian sausage, removed from casings and crumbled

1 cup sliced mushrooms

1 tbsp. extra-virgin olive oil

½ recipe basic pizza sauce (page 74)

1 cup shredded mozzarella

2 tbsp. unsalted butter, melted

4 tsp. finely grated parmesan cheese

Makes 4 calzoni

1 Preheat oven to maximum setting up to 450°F (230°C).

2 Prepare the calzone dough by combining two cups of the flour with the sugar, yeast, and salt in a bowl or mixer. Set aside. Combine the olive oil and warm water. Using the paddle attachment, slowly stir the water and oil into the flour mixture until well combined. Mix in one cup of flour.

3 Change to a dough hook attachment and knead on low for 4–5 minutes, until the dough comes together as a ball and is smooth and elastic. If you're not using a mixer, turn onto a lightly floured surface and knead by hand for about ten minutes. Put the dough in a lightly oiled bowl and cover with a clean paper towel. Set aside for 10 minutes.

4 When the dough has rested for ten minutes, punch it down. Using a sharp knife, cut the dough into four equal pieces. Shape each into a ball, flatten down to form a disc, and lightly flour each disc.

5 While the dough is resting, prepare the filling. Brown the crumbled sausage meat and mushroom slices in olive oil for five minutes, until the sausage is cooked through. Add pizza sauce.

6 On a lightly floured surface, roll out each disc an eighth of an inch thick and six inches round. Add flour as necessary to prevent sticking. Using a pastry brush, glaze the top edge of the circles with water. Spoon a quarter of the filling onto the lower half of each circle. Sprinkle with ¼ cup mozzarella. Fold the top over so that the edge of the top sits half an inch away from the bottom half. Lightly glaze the edge of the top piece and fold the bottom over to seal tightly. Make a half-inch slit in the top to allow steam to escape.

Brush the tops with melted butter and sprinkle with one teaspoon of parmesan. Put the calzoni on a preheated baking stone or on a cookie sheet lined with parchment paper and bake on the middle rack for 15–20 minutes, or until the filling is hot and the crust is golden brown.

Broiled chicken and fontina pizza

Fontina has a mildly fruity, nutty taste. The very best fontina comes from the Val d'Aosta, the tiny alpine region of northwestern Italy. It is made from unpasteurized milk and the fontina name is protected by Italian law.

~ Ingredients ~

1 recipe basic pan pizza crust (page 73)
½ recipe basic pizza sauce (page 74)
2 cups grated fontina cheese
2 cups broiled and sliced chicken breasts
2 thin slices red onion, rings separated
freshly ground black pepper
2 tbsp. finely chopped flat-leaf parsley
4 tbsp. finely grated parmesan

Serves 4

1 Follow the instructions on page 73 for making two round pizza crusts.

2 Preheat the oven to maximum setting, up to 550°F (300°C). Divide sauce between the two pans and spread thinly and evenly, leaving a half-inch border around the edge.

3 Spread one cup grated fontina over the sauce on each pizza. Arrange half the onion rings and one cup chicken on each pizza. Lightly sprinkle each one with pepper.

4 Bake for 8–10 minutes on the middle rack in the oven, until the cheese is melted and the crust is golden brown. Sprinkle chopped parsley and parmesan over the pizze.

5 Slice into wedges and serve.

Steak and mushroom pizza

84

Prep Time:
3 hours

Cooking Time:
10 mins

Steak and mushroom pizza

The steak on this pizza is best lightly broiled so that it is still rare. Use flank or sirloin steak if possible, and slice it thinly.

∽ Ingredients ∾

1 recipe basic pizza dough (page 73)
1 recipe pizza sauce (page 74)
12 oz. lightly broiled steak
(flank or sirloin), thinly sliced
8 oz. mushrooms, thinly sliced
1 cup shredded mozzarella
1 cup grated smoked gruyère
½ tsp. dried oregano (optional)

Serves 6–8

1 Follow the instructions on page 73 for making two round pizza crusts.

2 Preheat the oven to maximum setting, up to 550°F (300°C). Divide sauce between the two pans and spread evenly, leaving a half-inch border around the edge. Arrange steak and mushroom slices on both pizze.

3 Combine grated cheeses and divide evenly between the two pans.

4 Bake for 8–10 minutes on a rack in the lower half of the oven, until the cheese is melted and the crust is golden brown. Sprinkle with oregano if desired.

5 Slice into wedges and serve.

Prep Time:
3 hours

Cooking Time:
5 mins

Vegetarian pizza

Overflowing with fresh tomatoes, mushrooms, onions, peppers, and green and black olives, this pizza is a vegetable lover's dream.

~ Ingredients ~

1 recipe basic pizza dough (page 73)
1 recipe pizza sauce (page 74)
2 cups shredded mozzarella
2–3 vine-ripened tomatoes, sliced
1 cup sliced mushrooms
1 yellow onion, thinly sliced
1 green bell pepper, thinly sliced
½ cup sliced manzanilla olives
½ cup sliced black olives

Serves 2–4

1 Follow the instructions on page 73 for making a rectangular pizza crust.

2 Preheat the oven to maximum setting, up to 550°F (300°C). Spread the sauce evenly over the pizza crust, leaving a half-inch border around the edge. Put on the bottom rack in the oven and bake for eight minutes.

3 Remove from the oven and spread the shredded mozzarella evenly over the sauce. Arrange the fresh tomato, mushroom, onion, pepper, and olive slices over the cheese. Return to the oven and bake for another 5–6 minutes, until the cheese has melted and the crust is golden brown.

4 Remove from the oven and let stand for two minutes. Slice into 12 squares and serve immediately.

Prep Time:
3 hours
Cooking Time:
15 mins

Pizza siciliana

This very simple pizza, which has been prepared in this way for centuries, has bold, direct flavors and is far lighter than some of the deep-dish pizze, piled high with dozens of toppings.

∼ Ingredients ∼

½ quantity pizza dough (page 73)
¾ cup tomato sauce (page 74)
4 tomatoes, skinned and sliced
½ tsp. oregano
salt and ground black pepper
⅓ cup grated parmesan cheese
1 can anchovies
½ cup pitted black olives

Serves 2–4

1 Preheat the oven to maximum setting, up to 425°F (220°C). Shape the dough into a rectangular shape 12 x 8 inches, or use a fluted flan tin or large jelly roll tin.

2 Paint the dough with a pastry brush dipped in olive oil and then cover the surface with the tomato sauce.

3 Put the sliced tomatoes on top and sprinkle with oregano and seasoning.

4 Sprinkle with parmesan cheese.

5 Drain the can of anchovies and arrange the halved fillets in a lattice design. Put an olive in the center of each lattice.

6 Paint over with olive oil and bake for 15 minutes. Turn the heat down to 375°F (190°C) and bake for ten minutes more.

Polenta

Polenta—a thick maize porridge—was for centuries a staple food of northern Italy. Although pasta has become hugely popular there since the 1950s, a bowl of golden, grainy polenta remains the accompaniment of choice for stewed, braised, and roasted game birds or meats. Use with strong flavors and sauces.

~ Ingredients ~

3¾ cups coarse-grained polenta (cornmeal)
salt to taste

Serves 4–6

1 Bring 7½ cups water to a boil in a heavy saucepan (polenta tends to stick to thin pans). Turn the water down to a simmer.

2 Pour the meal to run into the water in a very thin stream, stirring continuously.

3 Once all the grain has been added, keep stirring. This is a job that will take 20 minutes.

4 Like couscous, the polenta is cooked when it can be lifted away from the sides of the pan as you stir. It should easily hold the shape of the spoon. Just before it reaches this point, add salt.

5 Either serve the polenta immediately, very hot, or pour it out into a shallow dish. When cooled and set (this takes about 2–3 hours), it can be sliced and further transformed.

6 Serve with cold meat and olives, or drizzle over a tomato sauce, season and top with cheese.

Pizza romana

Polenta was used as a topping for pizza in hard times when other ingredients weren't available—just as breadcrumbs were scattered over pasta in place of cheese. Even in good times, this pizza is worth eating. The cheese, polenta, and sauce combine to make a tasty and hearty meal.

❧ Ingredients ❧

½ quantity pizza dough (page 73)
½ cup polenta (cornmeal)
¼ tsp. salt
1 cup cold water
1 egg
1 oz. parmesan cheese, grated
½ cup pizza sauce (page 74)

Serves 2–4

1 Preheat the oven to maximum setting, up to 500°F (250°C).

2 Put the polenta and salt in a pan. Add the cold water a little at a time, whisking it in to remove all lumps. Put over moderate heat and continue whisking until the polenta thickens. When it gets too thick to whisk, switch to a wooden spoon. Continue stirring for about five minutes after the polenta thickens. Remove from the heat.

3 Beat the egg with four tablespoons of parmesan cheese. Stir into the polenta mixture.

4 To assemble the pizza, spread the pizza sauce over the pizza dough. Spread the polenta mixture on top of the sauce, using the back of a spoon to pat it down. Top with the remaining parmesan. Bake for ten minutes and serve hot.

Chicken and zucchini risotto

Prep Time:
15 mins

Cooking Time:
35 mins

Seek out the smallest zucchini possible for this risotto, as they have the most delicate flavor. The larger, more mature fruit tend to be a little watery. If you grow your own, pick the zucchini when they reach the size of your thumb.

❧ Ingredients ❧

3 cups chicken stock

2 tbsp. butter

1 tbsp. oil

8 chicken drumsticks

1 onion, finely chopped

2 garlic cloves, crushed

2 cups arborio rice

salt and ground black pepper

3 zucchini, grated

½ cup shelled pecan halves

¼ cup freshly grated parmesan cheese

Serves 4

1 Pour the stock into a saucepan and bring to a boil. Reduce the heat to a gentle simmer.

2 Meanwhile, melt the butter in a large skillet with the oil and gently cook the chicken for five minutes, turning until browned. Add the onion and garlic and cook for two minutes, stirring, until the onion has softened, but not browned. Stir in the rice and cook, stirring, for a further two minutes until the rice is well coated in butter.

3 Add a ladleful of stock to the rice and cook, stirring, until absorbed. Continue adding small quantities of stock to the rice until half of the stock has been used and the rice is creamy. Season and stir in the zucchini and pecans.

4 Continue adding the stock until the risotto becomes thick, but not sticky (about 25 minutes). Check that the chicken is cooked through and no pink remains in the center of the drumsticks. Stir in the parmesan cheese and serve in a warm bowl.

Walnut and garlic risotto

Walnuts are very popular in Italy, and are used in a number of distinctive ways— as a flavoring in alcoholic liqueurs; ground into a pasta sauce; and broken into chunks to decorate breads and cakes. The crunchy texture of small walnut pieces makes a good contrast to smooth, creamy risotto rice.

∽ Ingredients ∽

1 cup vegetable stock

2 tbsp. butter

1 tbsp. olive oil

4 cloves garlic, crushed

2⅓ cups very finely chopped walnuts

2 tbsp. chopped fresh thyme or chives

2 cups arborio rice

salt and freshly ground black pepper

1 tbsp. walnut oil

2⅓ cups walnut pieces

sprig fresh thyme or chives, to garnish

Serves 2

1 Pour the stock into a saucepan and bring to a boil. Reduce the heat to a gentle simmer.

2 Meanwhile, melt the butter with the oil in a large saucepan and gently fry the garlic, chopped walnuts and thyme for two minutes. Stir in the rice and cook, stirring, for a further two minutes until the rice is well-coated in the walnut mixture.

3 Add the stock, ladle by ladle, until all the liquid is absorbed and the rice is thick, creamy, and tender. Keep the heat moderate. This will take about 25 minutes and should not be hurried.

4 Adjust the seasoning and stir in the walnut oil. Serve the risotto sprinkled with the walnut pieces and garnished with thyme or chives.

Chicken and artichoke risotto

Prep Time:
15 mins

Cooking Time:
45 mins

Huge globe artichokes are a familiar sight at Italian markets, and there are numerous ways of enjoying the tender hearts. Combining their strong flavor with the subtler taste of chicken is a good way of encouraging eaters who are otherwise unsure about their quite distinctive flavor.

～ Ingredients ～

3½ cups chicken stock
½ cup dry white wine
¼ cup butter
1 tbsp. olive oil
4 boneless, skinned chicken breasts
1 onion, finely chopped
2 garlc cloves, crushed
2 cups arborio rice
salt and ground black pepper
juice of 1 lemon
1 celery stalk, chopped
8 artichokes in oil, drained and halved
2 tbsp. pimentos in brine, draind and cut into strips
3 tbsp. chopped fresh mixed herbs
3 tbsp. freshly grated parmesan cheese
fresh arugula to serve

1 Pour the stock and wine into a saucepan and bring to a boil. Reduce the heat to a gentle simmer.

2 Meanwhile, melt the butter in a large skillet with the oil and cook the chicken gently for five minutes, turning until browned. Add the onion and garlic and cook for two minutes, stirring, until the onion has softened but not browned. Stir in the rice and cook, stirring, for two minutes until the rice is well coated in butter.

3 Add a ladleful of stock and wine and cook gently, stirring, until all of the liquid has been absorbed. Continue adding small quantities of stock mixture until half of the stock has been used and the rice is creamy. Season and add the lemon juice and celery.

4 Continue adding stock for a further 20 minutes. Stir in the artichokes and pimientos. Continue cooking for a further five minutes, adding stock until the risotto is thick but not sticky. Just before serving, stir in the herbs and cheese and serve in a warm bowl.

5 Garnish with fresh arugula.

Serves 4

Gnocchi with gorgonzola

Prep Time:
10 mins

Cooking Time:
4 mins

Gnocchi can be made from potato or semolina dough; a lesser-known version from Friuli, in the mountains on the Slovenian border with Austria, uses breadcrumbs. This recipe for potato gnocchi with a creamy cheese sauce makes for a very filling dinner—perfect for cold nights when you want a big meal to enjoy with a glass of red wine.

∽ Ingredients ∽

1lb. potato gnocchi

salt

⅔ cup milk

4 tbsp. butter

¼ lb. Gorgonzola, crumbled into tiny pieces

2 tbsp. freshly grated parmesan cheese

4 tbsp. heavy cream

1 Boil the gnocchi as you would pasta, but keep an eye on them as they will cook more quickly—3–4 minutes should be quite sufficient.

2 As the gnocchi are cooking, heat the milk in a pan large enough to hold all the ingredients, including the gnocchi. As soon as the milk is warm, reduce the heat to a low simmer. Add the butter, the crumbled Gorgonzola, and the parmesan. Slowly beat everything into a creamy paste. Remove from the heat.

3 As soon as the gnocchi are cooked, drain them, and add them to the sauce. Over a very low heat, stir in the cream. Serve immediately.

Serves 4–6

Gnocchi with chicken livers

Prep Time: 10 mins

Cooking Time: 15 mins

Chicken livers can be meltingly tender if they are cooked gently until still pink inside. Combining them with plump little gnocchi makes for a comforting and satisfying winter supper.

⌇ Ingredients ⌇

1 lb. potato gnocchi

salt

2 tbsp. olive oil

2 cloves garlic

1 small onion, very finely chopped

¼ lb. fresh porcini mushrooms, sliced

1 tbsp. finely chopped fresh sage

½ lb. chicken livers

⅔ cup heavy cream

Serves 4–6

1 Cook the gnocchi in the usual manner (page 99).

2 Heat the oil in a skillet and throw in the whole cloves of garlic and the chopped onion. Soften in the oil until the onion begins to brown.

3 Add the mushrooms and cook for a further two minutes.

4 Add the sage and the red wine; reduce the volume of the wine by half over a high heat. Remove from the heat.

5 When all the gnocchi are ready, bring the red wine mixture back to a boil and toss in the livers, finely chopped. Cook for a minute or so, then add the cream. Bring the pan back to a boil. Check the seasoning and take the pan off the heat. Gently stir in the gnocchi and serve immediately.

Fried polenta with mushrooms

When polenta is left to cool, it solidifies into a thick slab that can be cut into wedges and fried or broiled, then dressed with a strongly flavored sauce. Italians are fond of thrifty dishes like this one, which use up food from the previous day's meal.

∽ Ingredients ∽

14 oz. button mushrooms
2 tbsp. flour
2 sprigs fresh sage
2 tbsp. oil for frying

For the polenta triangles:
1 clove garlic, peeled
salt and pepper
7 oz. polenta
oil for frying

Serves 6

1 Prepare the polenta according to the package instructions (page 90). Remove the pan from the heat, stir in one tbsp. olive oil and press in the garlic. Season with salt and pepper. Turn the hot polenta onto a smooth work surface or baking sheet and spread to a thickness of half an inch using a moistened spatula. Cover with a dish cloth and leave to go cold.

2 Clean and slice the mushrooms. Dust with a little flour and fry in oil on all sides for 2–4 minutes. Add a little chopped sage and fry briefly.

3 Cut the firm polenta into triangles and fry in oil on both sides until golden brown. Arrange on warmed plates, top with mushrooms, garnish with sage, and serve.

secondi piatti e contorni

The secondo would correspond in the eyes of American diners to the main course, consisting usually of a piece of fish or meat roast accompanied by contorni, or vegetable-based dishes, salads, or sides. Meat and fish can be prepared in a variety of ways: grilled, roasted, or baked; braised with vegetables; fried, as in the calamari fritti recipe, or boiled and served with a rich wine sauce, as in the Venetian-style tripe with chiles. Vegetables, when served as a side, are frequently just boiled and served at room temperature, to be drizzled with olive oil and lemon juice or marinated in olive oil. However, there are also many creative ways of cooking them, including the wonderful eggplant al carpione which, while originally eaten as a side dish, makes a fabulous vegetarian meal all on its own.

Sausages in tomato sauce with polenta

Prep Time: 3 hours

Cooking Time: 10 mins

Try to buy Italian sausages to use in this dish. They are often shorter and squatter than other varieties, with a high meat content. Especially flavorsome are the kind which combine ground pork and veal.

~ Ingredients ~

4 tbsp. olive oil

4 cloves garlic

1 medium onion, finely sliced

1 lb. fresh or canned plum tomatoes

¼ lb. chopped porcini mushrooms

⅔ cup dry white wine

1 chile

1½ lb. uncooked Italian sausages, sliced

3¾ cups polenta (page 90)

2 tbsp. finely chopped fresh basil

salt and freshly ground black pepper to taste

Serves 6

1 Heat the oil in a sturdy pan. Add the garlic and the finely sliced onion. Once the onions are soft, add the mushrooms. While the mushrooms are cooking, chop the tomatoes roughly. Add them when the mushrooms and onion are beginning to brown, and turn the heat up to medium-high.

2 Add the white wine and the chile, and bring the sauce to a boil. Turn to a low simmer, add the sliced sausages, and cover the pot.

3 As the sausages are braising, fry the polenta in a drop of olive oil.

4 The sausages and the polenta should be ready at the same time. Just before you serve them, add the finely chopped basil to the sausages and check the seasoning.

Trout al carpione

Preparing food al carpione—the nearest English translation is probably "soused"—is a popular way of dealing with meat, vegetables, and especially fish. The mildly acidic sauce has a crisp, refreshing flavor.

✌ Ingredients ✌

6 medium rainbow trout or 1 salmon rainbow trout (about 3¼ lb)

1 egg

1¼ cups olive oil

1 cup plain flour

1 large onion

4 cloves garlic

⅔ cup dry white wine

2 tbsp. vingear

2 tbsp. sugar

2 large sprigs fresh rosemary

4 fresh bay leaves

1 chile pepper

salt to taste

Serves 6

1 Clean and dry the fish.

2 Beat the egg and mix with an equal volume of water.

3 Heat about a third of the oil to a medium heat, dip the whole fish or slices of fish in the egg/water mixture and then roll in the flour. Fry gently until cooked the whole trout eight minutes per side, any slices half the time. When cooking the fish in this way, turn it only once.

4 Carefully remove the fish when it is cooked and arrange on a serving dish.

5 Set the rest of the olive oil on a medium heat. Slice the onion very finely and stew it in the oil. Add the garlic and cook both together until the onion is completely soft. Neither must brown.

6 Add the wine, vinegar, sugar, rosemary, bay leaves, and the whole chile. Bring everything to a boil and season. Pour the mixture over the fish and serve. This dish can be eaten warm, cool, or chilled.

Prep Time:
10 mins
Cooking Time:
20 mins

Calamari fritti

This dish needs to be prepared carefully if it is to avoid being rubbery and overcooked. Heat the oil until it is very hot indeed, and flash-fry the squid rings briefly so that they remain tender and tasty.

❧ Ingredients ❧

4½ lb. baby squid
2½ cups vegetable oil
1½ cups plain flour
salt and freshly ground black pepper
3 lemons, to serve
handful of lettuce leaves, to serve
fresh chives, to serve

Serves 6

1 Clean the squid. Slice the body sacs into rings.

2 Heat the oil until it is almost smoking.

3 Dip the squid in the flour, one batch at a time so the coating does not become soggy. Shake off the excess, and fry until light brown—about 30–40 seconds if the temperature is right. Set each batch to drain on paper towels.

4 Season when all is cooked and serve very hot on a bed of fresh lettuce, with the lemon cut into wedges. Garnish with fresh chives.

Pancetta-wrapped monkfish

Monkfish has a firm, dense texture and is often treated like meat. In Italian markets you might occasionally come across the whole fish, which is surprisingly ugly; elsewhere you'll only be able to buy the tails.

∾ Ingredients ∾

28 oz. monkfish fillet (1 large fillet)
2 tbsp. lemon juice
7 oz. pancetta, sliced very thinly
½ cup vegetable broth
1 small onion
10½ oz. fresh spinach
salt and freshly ground black pepper
2 tbsp. clarified butter
a little white wine
1 tbsp. olive oil

For the stuffing:
3 cloves garlic
1 bunch mixed herbs (dill, basil, parsley, and chives)
1 egg white

Serves 4

1 Cut the monkfish fillet lengthwise into strips an inch wide and sprinkle with one tablespoon of lemon juice. For the stuffing, wash the herbs and purée finely in a liquidizer or food processor with the peeled garlic. Mix with the egg white and spread on half of the strips of fish. Put the other strips on top and wrap firmly in pancetta.

2 Sort, wash, and drain the spinach. Peel the onion and chop very finely. Heat the broth in a pan, add the onion, and boil until reduced by half. Add the spinach, heat until it collapses and season to taste with salt and pepper.

3 Heat the clarified butter and fry the fish parcels lightly on all sides. Add enough white wine to cover the bottom of the pan, and steam in the closed pan until the fish is cooked.

4 Slice the fish and serve on plates with the spinach, drizzled with the remaining lemon juice and olive oil.

Baked seabass with mayonnaise

Prep Time: 1 hour

Cooking Time: 30 mins

Seabass is hugely popular in Italy, where it is farmed intensively. Although mostly a seawater fish, it sometimes strays from the Mediterranean into rivers, lagoons, and brackish freshwater. This recipe is a delicious preparation which retains all the flavor and juiciness of the fish.

∽ Ingredients ∽

1 seabass, about 3½ lb.
2 large onions
4 tbsp. olive oil
2 cloves garlic
2 sprigs fresh rosemary
2 tbsp. finely chopped fresh parsley
2 tbsp. finely chopped fresh basil
juice of 1 lemon
4 tbsp. dry white wine
salt and freshly ground black pepper
2 cups mayonnaise

Serves 6

1 Preheat oven to 350°F (180°C). Clean and descale the fish.

2 Very finely slice the onion and make a fish-shaped bed of it on a large piece of foil. Pour the olive oil over it and lay the fish on top.

3 Crush the garlic and smear along the inside of the fish. Lay the rosemary sprigs inside. Chop the parsley and basil finely, mix with the lemon juice, and smear along the inside.

4 Raise the edges of the foil, pour over the white wine, and season. Seal the parcel carefully, making sure there are no holes or tears.

5 Set the parcel in an amply sized dish and bake for 30 minutes. When ready, remove from the oven, but do not unseal until the parcel is completely cool. About 45 minutes before eating, remove the fish from its wrapper and collect all the juice into a small saucepan. Boil them down and let cool, then add them to the mayonnaise.

6 Garnish the fish with the onions on which it lay, and serve with salad and fresh bread.

Prep Time:
2 hours

Cooking Time:
30 mins

Italian broiled fish

You could use any fish here, with the only crucial factor being absolute freshness. If using mackerel, it would be best only to cook those you've caught yourself, so you can be sure they are extremely fresh.

∽ Ingredients ∽

6 whole fish, about 12 oz. each
½ cup olive oil
juice of 1 lemon
freshly ground black pepper
2 tbsp. fresh oregano
1 tbsp. very fine breadcrumbs
sea salt to taste

1 Clean, dry, and descale the fish, if necessary. Combine the oil and lemon juice and coat the fish thoroughly.

2 Combine the black pepper, oregano, breadcrumbs, and salt and rub into the fish. Let sit for about two hours.

3 Heat the broiler to maximum heat and cook the fish until cooked all the way through (about 30 minutes), turning only once.

Serves 6

salad of fresh tuna and bacon

Prep Time:
2 hours

Cooking Time:
10 mins

This dish is wonderful when accompanied by bitter radicchio. If possible, use a red radicchio to make the dish a beautiful contrast of shades of red and pink. Shred two heads of the lettuce and serve with the tuna and bacon salad on top.

∽ Ingredients ∽

2 lb. fresh tuna
1 lb. bacon or pancetta
4 tbsp. fresh oregano
⅔ cup olive oil
juice of 1 lemon
2 cloves garlic, well crushed
salt and freshly ground black pepper to taste
1½ tbsp. freshly grated parmesan cheese

Serves 4

1 Dice the tuna into thumb-size chunks. Lay the pancetta out in flat strips and spread it with the oregano, very finely chopped.

2 Lay a piece of tuna at the start of each bacon strip, roll in the bacon and pin with a toothpick. Continue in the same way down each strip until all the tuna is wrapped.

3 Combine the olive oil and lemon juice and add it to the garlic. Marinade the pinned pieces of tuna and bacon in the mixture for about two hours.

4 Pre-heat the broiler to its highest setting. Thread the bacon and fish chunks onto skewers. Imagine the skewers have four faces. Broil each face for two minutes.

5 Detach the fish from the skewers when cooked, then separate the fish and bacon. Finely chop the bacon pieces.

6 Dress the fish in the marinade, season and sprinkle over the bacon and parmesan. Serve warmish.

stuffed salmon or trout

Prep Time:
20 mins

Cooking Time:
35 mins

Oily fish like salmon and trout respond well to a gutsy stuffing like this anchovy and olive combination. It is strongly reminiscent of the flavors of southern Italy, which tend to be bolder and more rustic in their simplicity than the French-influenced dishes of the north.

⌐ Ingredients ⌐

1 small salmon or large salmon trout, about 4½ lb.

½ lb. fresh or canned plum tomatoes

4 tbsp. olive oil

4 cloves garlic

2 sprigs fresh rosemary

6 anchovy fillets

⅓ cup black olives

2 tbsp. white wine vinegar

4 tbsp. dry white wine

2 tbsp. brandy

salt and freshly ground black pepper

Serves 4

1 Preheat the oven to 350°F (180°C). Clean and descale the fish. Roughly chop the tomatoes and spread them out on a large sheet of foil. Mix the olive oil with the chopped tomatoes and lay the fish on top.

2 Crush the garlic and smear the inside of the fish with it. Lay the rosemary sprigs and anchovy fillets at regular intervals inside the cavity. Chop the olives very finely and sprinkle half inside, half outside.

3 Combine the wine vinegar and brandy and pour over the fish, then lift the sides of the foil and seal the fish carefully. Bake the fish for 35 minutes.

4 Lift the fish from the foil with a long fish slice when it is cooked. Take care when transferring it so that it does not break, and set it on a serving dish.

5 Pour all the juices from the foil into a pan and bring them to a rapid boil. Season with the salt and pepper, pour over the fish, and serve.

Braised squid with parsley stuffing

Braised squid with parsley stuffing

Prep Time: 20 mins

Cooking Time: 30 mins

This dish is best with small squid but the stuffing could be used to stuff fewer, larger squid. If those are the only ones available to you, increase the cooking time so that the flesh is not tough.

❧ Ingredients ❧

12 squid, each about 3¼ in. long

2 tbsp. finely chopped fresh parsley

2 cloves garlic, crushed

3 tbsp. freshly grated parmesan cheese

½ cup fresh breadcrumbs

2 anchovy fillets

1 egg

6 tbsp. olive oil

½ lb. fresh or canned plum tomatoes

½ cup dry white wine

1 chile pepper

salt to taste

1 Clean the squid, if this has not already been done. Finely chop the tentacles. Combine the parsley, garlic, and breadcrumbs. Mash and mix in the anchovy fillets. Beat the egg and mix it with the bread mixture. Add about half the oil and the squid tentacles. Push the mixture into the squid bodies, stopping about two thirds of the way down (the squid will shrink as it cooks and thus push the stuffing down to the end).

2 Heat the rest of the oil in a pan large enough to hold all the fish in one layer. Roughly chop the tomatoes and add them to the oil with the wine and the whole chile.

3 Bring the tomatoes and wine to a boil, then turn the heat to a very low simmer. Add the squid and seal the pan tightly. Cook for about 30 minutes, until a fork will easily pierce the squid. Season the sauce and wait, if you like—the dish may be served hot, warm, or cold.

Serves 6

Broiled scampi

Prep Time:
15 mins
Cooking Time:
15 mins

Broiled scampi

Scampi is the Italian name for langoustines. They are the same size as large Mediterranean shrimp, but are distinguishable by their prominent claws. On no account buy precooked langoustines.

∽ Ingredients ∽

24 large scampi
¼ pt. olive oil
juice of 1 lemon
3 tbsp. freshly grated parmesan cheese
½ cup fresh breadcrumbs
sea salt

Serves 4

1 Cut the fish in half lengthwise, leaving a thin strip of shell at the back so the two pieces remain just about attached.

2 Combine half the oil and the lemon juice and brush each shrimp with the mixture. Combine the cheese and the breadcrumbs and sprinkle over the exposed flesh. Sprinkle the shrimp with the remaining oil and dot with sea salt.

3 Preheat the broiler to maximum and broil until the cheese forms a light brown crust. Serve immediately with a wedge of lemon.

Pigeon breasts with pine nuts

The feral pigeons that breed in urban areas across the Western hemisphere have rather dented the image of the pigeon as foodstuff. However, farmed or wild pigeons of other varieties yield a delicious, rich meat, considered a delicacy in France, Italy, Morocco, and other Mediterranean countries.

⚜ Ingredients ⚜

6 young pigeons
⅓ cup olive oil
⅓ cup pine nuts
4 tbsp. olive oil
juice and zest of 1 lemon
⅔ cup Marsala

Serves 4

1 Remove the breasts from the pigeons. Keeping the blade very close to the high-ridged breast bone, a swift stroke of the knife from back to front will have the breast hanging on by skin only. Cut through the skin.

2 Heat the olive oil in a very large pan. Roughly chop the carcasses and add them to the pan, cover with water and bring to a boil. Allow to simmer.

3 In a skillet containing no oil, toast the pine nuts until they begin to brown.

4 Heat the olive oil in a heavy pan and drop in each pigeon breast. Cook for no more than ten seconds on each side. The breasts will puff up. Remove the skin and then slice each breast through across the horizontal plane. Seal the raw sides of each breast for a further 2–3 seconds in the hot oil.

5 Pour away most of the oil and return the pan to a high heat. Add the lemon juice, zest, and the Marsala and reduce until you have a thick syrup, about 5 minutes. Stir in ⅔ cup of the pigeon broth made from the carcasses and reduce again.

6 Toss the breasts into the sauce and reheat for half a minute. Remove the breasts from the pan, pour the sauce over them, and sprinkle the browned pine nuts on top.

Braised pheasant

Prep Time:
30 mins

Cooking Time:
2½ hours

Pheasant is sometimes too tough to benefit from standard roasting, so Italians have evolved a wet-roast technique that tenderizes the meat beautifully. Use a dish into which the birds fit snugly.

∽ Ingredients ∽

2 pheasants
4 tbsp. olive oil
1 medium onion, finely sliced
2 cloves garlic
8 sprigs fresh rosemary
4 tbsp. Marsala
4 tbsp. brandy
½ cup dry white wine
salt and freshly ground black pepper

Serves 4

1 Preheat oven to 325°F (160°C). Cut away the backbones from the pheasants, then slice each bird into two.

2 In a tray large enough to hold the pheasant halves side by side, heat the oil. Soften the finely sliced onion. Throw the garlic in whole. As the onion cooks, flatten out the pheasants as much as possible—either press with the palm of your hand or work them with the flat of a meat cleaver.

3 Lay the sprigs of rosemary on top of the softened onions, then lay the pheasant breasts down on top of that. Cook for 2–3 minutes on a high flame.

4 Take a fork and liberally prick the upper and still uncooked sides of the birds. Mix the Marsala and brandy together and pour an equal amount over each bird. Cover the dish very tightly and put in the oven.

5 After 1½ hours' cooking, turn the birds, scooping all the onion and rosemary you can on top of the breasts. Now add the white wine. Return once more to the oven and continue cooking until the pheasants are very tender—about an hour more.

6 Season the pan juices at the last minute and pour on top of the birds. Serve with roasted vegetables.

Prep Time:
30 mins

Cooking Time:
1½ hours

Rabbit with onions

Italians tend to be unsentimental about food, and rabbit remains an extremely popular meat in Italy while other nations have grown slightly squeamish about eating it. Farmed rabbit has a pleasant, mild flavor, and it is delicious with this sauce of soft, sweet onions.

∼ Ingredients ∼

1 large rabbit, weighing about 2 lb.
4 tbsp. olive oil
3 large onions
6 cloves garlic
6 bay leaves
3 chile peppers
4 sprigs fresh rosemary
4 tbsp. brandy
salt and freshly ground black pepper

Serves 4

1 Preheat the oven to 350°F (180°C). Cut away the legs from the rabbit carcass and joint each one at the knee. Cut the saddle into four pieces: haunch, belly, and ribcage split in two along the breastbone.

2 Heat the oil over medium heat and brown the rabbit pieces for 3–4 minutes. Remove them from the pan with a slotted spoon and set aside.

3 Slice the onions very finely and add them to the pan in which you browned the rabbit. Increase the heat and cook them until they begin to color. Reduce the heat and add the whole garlic cloves, whole chile peppers, and the rosemary sprigs. Return the rabbit to the pan and smother with the onions. Cover tightly and begin baking.

4 After about an hour, completely turn all the contents, add the brandy, and season. Continue cooking until the rabbit is very tender—another 30 minutes or so.

Roast chicken with rosemary

Try to use a fine-flavored free-range or organic chicken, as the meat is really superior to factory-farmed birds. The aroma of roasting chicken, garlic, and rosemary will fill your kitchen as the chicken roasts—truly mouthwatering.

⌣ Ingredients ⌣

1 roasting chicken
(about 2½–3 lb.)

4 cloves garlic

4 good sprigs fresh rosemary

⅔ cup olive oil

4 tbsp. dry white wine

salt to taste

Serves 4

1 Preheat the oven to 375°F (190°C). Put the chicken in a roasting tin, crush the garlic and smear it around the cavity of the chicken, and put two sprigs of rosemary inside with it, then chop the remainder and sprinkle it over and around the bird with the oil. Put in the oven.

2 The chicken will be cooked in an hour or so, but baste it thoroughly with the pan juices every 15 minutes.

3 When cooked, let the bird rest for five minutes. Skim the oil off the pan juices and set the dish over a very hot flame. Add the wine and bring everything to a rapid boil. Season, pour over the chicken, and serve.

Prep Time:
15 mins

**Cooking
Time:**
40 mins

Braised chicken

This is a dish that is remarkably easy to spoil if you do not trust its simplicity and start to elaborate. The whole point of it is that the chicken cooks in its own juices, flavored simply by the peppers. No onions, and no other broth. The bacon on top keeps the meat moist.

∽ Ingredients ∾

1 roasting chicken, about 3 lb.

4 tbsp. olive oil

4 red bell peppers

4 cloves garlic

4 chile peppers

½ lb. bacon or pancetta

salt to taste

Serves 4

1 Cut the chicken into four serving pieces, or have the butcher do this for you. Heat the oil in your heaviest casserole dish—one with a close-fitting lid—and thoroughly brown the chicken pieces. Remove them from the heat.

2 Seed the bell peppers and cut them into fine strips. Cook in the chicken oil until soft, about ten minutes. Return the chicken pieces to the pan, smothering them with the peppers.

3 Add the whole garlic cloves and chile peppers. Lay the strips of bacon over everything, cover the pan, and cook at a very low heat until the chicken is tender—about 30 minutes.

4 Season lightly with the salt (remember that because of the bacon, you will need very little).

Cotechino with lentils

Prep Time:
20 mins

Cooking Time:
3 hours

Cotechino is a fresh pork sausage from Modena; you will need to find a specialty butcher or Italian food store to buy it. This dish is a traditional New Year dinner for northern Italians, and is often served alongside polenta.

Ingredients

1 cotechino sausage
2 tbsp. olive oil
4 cloves garlic
1 medium onion, roughly chopped
4 tbsp. tomato paste
½ cup red wine
2 tbsp. chopped fresh sage
1 cup green lentils
salt and pepper to taste

Serves 6

1 Soak the sausage in cold water for at least four hours, or overnight. About three hours before you're ready to eat, set the sausage to boil, whole and unpricked, in plenty of water—at least five pints—and start from cold. Simmer until tender, about 2½ hours.

2 With an hour to go, heat the olive oil to near smoking in a heavy pan. Throw in the garlic, unchopped, and the onion. Cook the onion until it begins to catch around the edges, then drop the flame to low. While the pan is still hot, add the tomato paste, red wine, and sage, and stir well. Let the sage infuse in the liquids for three minutes. Add the lentils and again stir well.

3 Pour in water to cover the lentils by one inch and cook on a low simmer until tender, about 40 minutes. Keep checking the water content. Add more to cover the lentils if you have to.

4 When the lentils are tender, let them stand to absorb whatever remains in the pot. They should be coated with a thick, moist sheen, but should not be swimming. If there is too much liquid, increase the heat and boil it off. Season to taste.

5 Remove the cotechino from its broth when cooked. Slice it and serve on top of the lentils.

Beef braised in Barolo

Barolo, from Piedmont, is one of the finest red wines in the world, a true delight for connoisseurs, who relish its pine and tar aroma. However, it is also very expensive. Feel free to substitute any rich, strong red wine in this dish.

～ Ingredients ～

2 tbsp. olive oil
1 beef joint of about 2 lb.
1 cup olive oil
1¼ cups Barolo or Chianti
1¼ cups broth (use beef
broth cube)
2 oz. fresh or canned plum tomatoes
¼ oz. each of thyme and marjoram
salt to taste

Serves 4

1 Preheat the oven 350°F (180°C). Heat the oil on a medium flame on the stove and brown the joint of beef. Seal it in every possible place then set it aside.

2 Now add the olive oil to the beef pan and cook it until soft, about four minutes.

3 Transfer the beef to a casserole a little larger than the beef itself. Drizzle the oil over and around the beef. Pour in the wine, the broth, and the tomatoes; add the herbs.

4 Put the beef in the oven, covered with a well-fitting lid. Turn the joint completely over half way through (after about ten minutes).

5 To serve, carve the joint and spoon the sauce over.

Fillet of beef with orange

Fillet of beef with orange

Prep Time:
5 mins

Cooking Time:
2 mins

Marsala and bitter oranges are both key ingredients of the Sicilian kitchen. Use a Marsala marked "superiore" if possible—these have been aged for at least two years, whereas those branded "fine" have been produced more quickly.

∽ Ingredients ∽

1 tbsp. olive oil

4 fillet steaks, each weighing about 6 oz.

4 tbsp. Marsala

4 tbsp. red wine

2 seville oranges

salt

a generous amount of coarsely ground black pepper

1 red onion, sliced

1 cup arugula

Serves 4

1 Heat the oil in a heavy skillet. Brown the steaks for a minute on each side. Retrieve them from the pan and set them aside in a warm place (a very low oven will do). Over a very high heat, add the Marsala and red wine to deglaze the pan.

2 Lower the heat, zest the oranges, and add both juice and zest to the pan.

3 If you prefer your meat medium, return the steaks to the pan and reheat them as the juices reduce. For rare steaks, cook the wine and juice down to a consistency of light syrup before you return the meat.

4 To serve, pour the juices over each steak. Sprinkle with salt and a generous amount of black pepper before eating. Serve with the arugula and onion slices.

Tripe with chiles

Boiled tripe dressed with vinegar is the most familiar way of serving this variety meat, but it deserves a more refined treatment: here the porcini and wine make a rich sauce, and the tripe responds surprisingly well to the spicy chiles.

∽ Ingredients ∽

2 lb. honeycomb tripe
4 tbsp. olive oil
4 cloves garlic, chopped
1 medium onion, chopped
1 lb. fresh or canned plum tomatoes, roughly chopped
½ cup dry white wine
1 oz. dried porcini, rinsed, and dried
4 chile peppers
1 sprig fresh rosemary
2 anchovy fillets
salt and pepper to taste
parmesan cheese (optional)

Serves 6

1 Bring ten cups of water to a boil and plunge the tripe into it. Boil for 30 minutes. As the tripe is cooking, heat the oil, soften the garlic and onions together in it, and add the tomatoes, wine, porcini, and half a cup water. Bring everything to a boil.

2 As the sauce is warming, slice and seed two chiles. Add all chile pieces, the rosemary, and the anchovy fillets to the sauce. When it boils, turn the heat to a very low simmer and cover.

3 When the tripe has boiled for 30 minutes, remove it, and slice very finely. Add it to the sauce and cook until tender enough to cut with a fork—about an hour. Season and serve with shavings of parmesan.

spinach and ham omelet

Prep Time:
10 mins

Cooking Time:
20 mins

Technically, this dish is a frittata, not an omelet. Italian frittate are quite different to the more familiar French version: they are served open, rather than folded, and are broiled to finish cooking and brown the top. A popular filling in Naples is leftover spaghetti—well worth trying. You could improvise other combinations of vegetables, cheeses, and meats.

⌒ Ingredients ⌒

6 eggs
3 tbsp. freshly grated parmesan cheese
4 oz. Parma ham, roughly chopped
6 oz. cooked spinach
salt and pepper to taste
4 tbsp. olive oil

1 Thoroughly beat the eggs. Mix in the cheese, Parma ham, spinach, salt, and pepper.

2 Heat the oil over a medium heat in a heavy skillet. Pour in the mixture, then turn the heat down as low as it will go. Cover the pan and cook until everything is set—about 20 minutes.

3 Serve at whatever temperature you wish.

Serves 2

Prep Time:
15 mins

Cooking Time:
30 mins

Sweetbreads

Sweetbreads are a meltingly tender variety meat, regarded as a real delicacy by Italian cooks. They can be chopped finely to make a stuffing or mashed into a smooth pâté—or poached with aromatic herbs, as here.

∾ Ingredients ∾

1 carrot, roughly chopped

1 stick celery, roughly chopped

2 small onions

½ lemon

1½ lb sweetbreads

5 tbsp. olive oil

1 cup dry white wine

¾ lb. shelled garden peas, fresh or frozen

1 sprig fresh rosemary

1 chile pepper

salt and freshly ground black pepper to taste

Serves 4–6

1 Bring seven cups of water to a boil and add the roughly chopped carrot and celery, one of the onions, and the half lemon. Poach the sweetbreads in this court bouillon for 5 minutes.

2 Remove the sweetbreads. You will now clearly see the membrane around them. Carefully remove as much of this as you can, and set the sweetbreads aside.

3 Heat the olive oil over medium heat. Finely slice the other onion and sauté it in the oil. Add the sweetbreads, sliced into one inch chunks, and brown them over medium heat with the onions for about four minutes. Add the white wine, the garden peas (if using fresh ones), the rosemary, and the whole chile. Cover the pot and poach the sweetbreads for 15–20 minutes.

4 Remove the sweetbreads and set them aside.

5 Over very high heat, reduce the cooking liquid until there will be just enough to glaze the sweetbreads. Return them to the pan, with the frozen garden peas, if using.

6 Season and serve as soon as everything is hot.

Bucatini with tomatoes

Prep Time:
15 mins

Cooking Time:
30 mins

Bucatini—from the Italian word *bucato*, meaning pierced—are spaghetti-like pasta with a thin hole running through the center. They are especially popular in Lazio, the region around Rome, where they are often served with *salsa amatriciana*, made from pancetta, tomatoes, and chile. This is a vegetarian version of that sauce. You could use parmesan cheese if pecorino is not available.

⌒ Ingredients ⌒

1 lb. dried bucatini
1 tbsp. olive oil
2 cloves garlic, crushed
1 onion, finely chopped
3 cups puréed tomatoes
4 tbsp. chopped fresh basil
salt and freshly ground black pepper
butter, for greasing
⅔ cup freshly grated pecorino

Serves 4

1 Bring a large saucepan of water to a boil. Add the bucatini and olive oil. Cook for about ten minutes or until al dente. Drain and set aside.

2 Preheat the oven to 400°F (200°C). Put the garlic, onion, tomatoes, basil, and seasoning in a large skillet, and heat until simmering. Cook for about five minutes, then remove from the heat.

3 Arrange the bucatini in a shallow, buttered ovenproof dish into which they fit tightly. Curl the pasta around to fit the dish. Spoon the tomato mixture over the top, prodding the pasta to ensure the sauce sinks down to the bottom of the dish. Sprinkle with the grated cheese and bake for 25–30 minutes, until bubbling, crisp, and golden. Cut in wedges, like a cake, to serve.

Eggplant al carpione

Prep Time: 20 mins

Cooking Time: 15 mins

This dish is traditionally served as a contorno, or side dish, but it makes a very special vegetarian main course, too. Charring eggplant is the best way to release its smoky flavor and to relieve any hint of sliminess in the texture.

~ Ingredients ~

1¼ cups olive oil

1 large onion

4 cloves garlic

⅔ cup dry white wine

4 tbsp. vinegar

2 tbsp. sugar

2 large sprigs fresh rosemary

4 fresh bay leaves

1 chile pepper

2 medium eggplants

salt to taste

mozzarella or parmesan cheese (optional)

Serves 4

1 Put half the olive oil in a pan and set it over medium heat.

2 Slice the onion finely and stew in the oil. Add the garlic and cook both together until the onion is soft. It must not color.

3 Add the wine, vinegar, sugar, rosemary, bay leaves, and the whole chile. Bring the mixture to a boil, then remove it from the heat and season it. Reserve.

4 Cut the eggplants into slices and fry them in batches in the remaining oil over high-ish heat. Cook them until they wrinkle and brown.

5 Set each batch to drain on paper towels as you prepare the next.

6 When all eggplant is cooked, arrange it in a dish. Simply pour the wine and oil mixture over it.

7 For extra flavor, add some mozzarella or parmesan cheese, and allow to melt: a simply mouthwatering accompaniment.

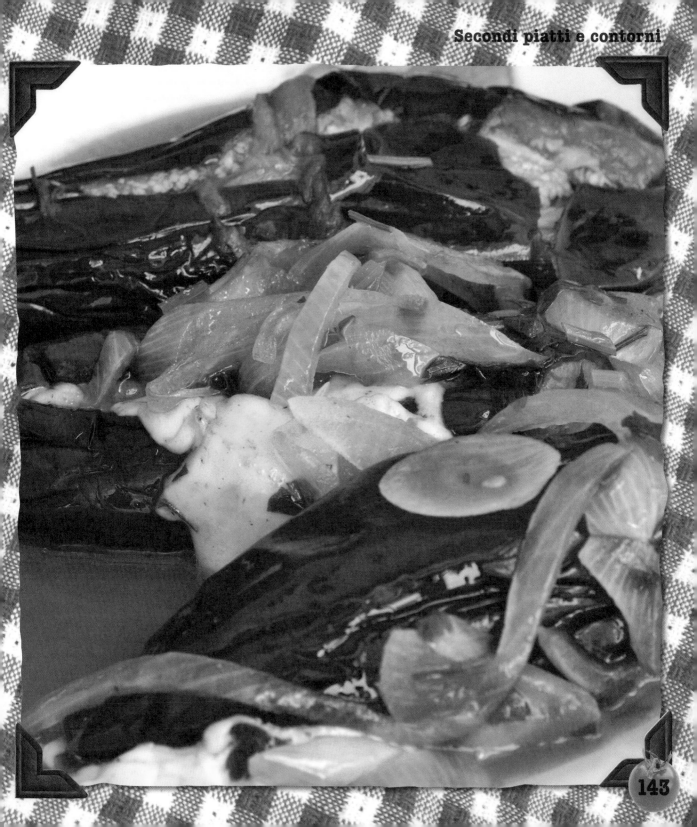

Baked eggplant with mozzarella

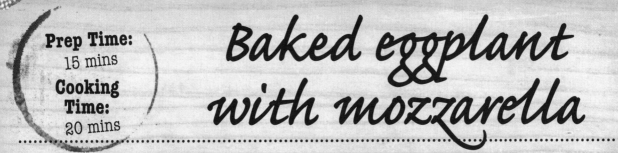

Baked eggplant with mozzarella

This dish, called *melanzane alla parmigiana*, is not—as you might think from the name—from Parma, nor is it named after the parmesan cheese that it features. In fact, this dish originated in Sicily: the first place in Europe where eggplants were widely enjoyed, after their introduction by Arabs in the Middle Ages. Many of the best Italian eggplant dishes come from the island. The same cooking method and topping can be used for veal and chicken.

∿ Ingredients ∿

2 medium eggplants
4 tbsp. olive oil
1 lb. fresh or canned plum tomatoes
2 tbsp. fresh oregano (half the quantity for dried)
salt and freshly ground black pepper
½ lb. mozzarella cheese
3 tbsp. freshly grated parmesan cheese

Serves 4

1 Preheat the oven to 400°F (200°C). Cut off the coarse stalks of the eggplants and slice them lengthwise in half-inch slices. Bake the slices in the oven, directly on the wire shelving, for ten minutes or until very soft.

2 In the meantime, oil a baking dish. Chop the tomatoes roughly and combine with the oregano. Season strongly with salt and pepper. Grate the mozzarella and mix it with the parmesan.

3 Remove the eggplant slices from the oven and line the baking dish with one layer. Spread the tomato and oregano mixture evenly over it, and sprinkle the mozzarella and parmesan as a final, thick coating: the cheese will melt and seal the dish as it cooks.

4 Bake until the cheese melts and browns (approximately 15–20 minutes).

Prep Time:
10 mins

Cooking Time:
10 mins

spinach with oil, lemon, and pepper

This dish is best made with small, tender leaves of baby spinach. If using the tougher, older leaves, trim away the stalks so that the overall texture of the finished dish is soft and smooth.

∾ Ingredients ∾

2 lb. fresh spinach
⅔ cup olive oil, plus extra for greasing
juice of half a lemon
salt and a copious quantity of freshly ground black pepper

Serves 4–6

1 Trim the stalks from the spinach leaves.

2 Very lightly oil the bottom of a thick pan and set in on a low heat. Introduce the spinach a little at a time. It will shrink as it comes in contact with the heat. Cover the pan and steam the spinach for about ten minutes over a fairly low heat.

3 When the spinach is cooked, press it lightly in a colander and secure the juices for another use. Allow the spinach to cool slightly. Then simply dress it with the olive oil, lemon juice, salt, and pepper.

4 Eat it hot, warm, or cool.

Milanese-style fennel

Prep Time:
20 mins

Cooking Time:
20 mins

Many foods are delicious when coated in breadcrumbs and fried. The best are those which offer a fresh, crisp flavor in contrast to the rich, oily batter. Fennel is sublime in this way, as its aniseed taste is highly refreshing.

∽ Ingredients ∾

3 medium fennel bulbs

⅔ cup white wine

2 tbsp. vinegar

1 clove garlic

2 bay leaves

salt to taste

2 eggs

3 cups fresh breadcrumbs

⅔ cup olive oil

1 lime (optional)

Serves 4–6

1 Cut the fennel into wedges from the root upward.

2 Put the wedges, with the white wine, vinegar, garlic, and bay leaves, into 3 cups water, and bring everything to a boil. Salt the liquid to taste and poach the fennel wedges in it for 10–15 minutes or until soft. Drain the fennel and pat it dry.

3 In a shallow bowl, beat the eggs well. Dip each fennel piece into the egg, covering it well. Shake off any excess. Now press the fennel wedges forcefully into the breadcrumbs—spread out on an open surface to make it easier to do.

4 Heat the oil to a fast-frying temperature; fry each piece of fennel until crisp on both sides. Eat hot and serve with optional lime wedges.

Mushrooms in garlic and parsley

Prep Time:
10 mins

Cooking Time:
5 mins

Italian has a verb meaning "to fry with garlic and parsley"—*trifolare*.
You will come across a number of things that are trifolati, notably *funghi*
(as here) and zucchini. Use wild mushrooms rather than cultivated button
mushrooms (or a mixture of the two) if at all possible.

∿ Ingredients ∿

1½ lb. good mushrooms
4 tbsp. olive oil
3 cloves garlic, crushed
2 tbsp. chopped fresh parsley
salt and freshly ground black pepper
to taste

Serves 6

1 Wash but do not peel the mushrooms. Slice or chop them into thumb-sized chunks if they are particularly large.

2 Heat the oil to medium and saute the crushed garlic for 30 seconds or so. Add the mushrooms. These will absorb the oil very quickly. When they do, turn down the heat and wait for the process to reverse—the mushrooms begin to give off their own liquid. This will take about two minutes.

3 Increase the heat and add the parsley, salt, and pepper. Cook on for a further 2–3 minutes and serve.

Tomato, onion, and basil omelet

Here is another frittata prepared in the same way as the spinach and ham version on page 138. In Italy, the best basil is grown on the sunny cliffsides of Liguria, the coastal strip by the French border, which is the home of pesto. Basil grown in more temperate climates will not have the same warm, spicy aroma, but will still taste good here. Just be sure not to cook it too fiercely: It should wilt, not fry, or it will turn bitter.

⌒ Ingredients ⌒

4 tbsp. olive oil
1 medium onion, finely chopped
½ lb. fresh or canned plum tomatoes
3 tbsp. roughly chopped fresh basil
6 eggs
3 tbsp. freshly grated parmesan cheese
salt and pepper to taste

Serves 4

1 Heat a little over half the oil in a heavy pan. Add the onions and cook until soft—about 3–4 minutes.

2 As the onions are cooking, roughly chop the tomatoes. Add them when the onions are ready. Turn up the heat and reduce the pan liquids by a good third.

3 Toss in the roughly chopped basil and remove the pan from the heat.

4 In a bowl, beat the eggs thoroughly. Add the cheese, fold the tomato mixture into the eggs and season well. Replace the pan on the heat, and pour in the remaining oil.

5 Scrape the egg and tomato mixture into the pan, turn the heat down very low and cover. Cook unil everything is set, about 20 minutes.

6 Serve at any temperature except chilled.

Broiled tomato salad with peppers

152

Broiled tomato salad with peppers

Prep Time:
10 mins
Cooling Time:
1 hour

This is a very versatile vegetable dish that could be served simply with crusty bread for a light lunch, or as a side dish with broiled fish or meat. Similar broiled salads are popular around the Mediterranean; you could vary this one by adding strips of broiled eggplant or zucchini, or topping it with poached eggs.

∾ Ingredients ∾

1¼ lb. firm, but ripe,
well-flavored tomatoes
1 red bell pepper
1 yellow bell pepper
6 tbsp. olive oil
1½ tbsp. mild red wine vinegar
1 garlic clove, crushed
salt and pepper

1 Preheat the barbecue or broiler.

2 Broil the tomatoes and peppers, turning frequently, until evenly charred and blistered. Let cool enough to handle and then peel them.

3 Slice the tomatoes. Cut the peppers in half and discard the cores and seeds; then slice the flesh.

4 Mix together the tomatoes and peppers. Whisk together the oil, vinegar, garlic, and seasoning, pour over the vegetables and leave for about an hour.

Serves 4

Asparagus risotto

Prep Time: 15 mins

Cooking Time: 30 mins

Few risotti are as elegant as this one, provided that you use only slender young asparagus spears and remove the woody bottom sections from thicker, older asparagus. The finest risotto rice is vialone nano, grown in paddy fields in the Veneto region inland from Venice. You could use carnaroli or arborio rice if you prefer—just be sure that you have a short-grain variety suitable for risotto.

∾ Ingredients ∾

8 oz. asparagus spears
1 cup vegetable broth
1 tbsp. olive oil
1 medium onion, finely chopped
2 cups arborio rice
4 tbsp. extra-dry vermouth
4 tbsp. double cream
salt and freshly ground black pepper
2½ tbsp. freshly grated parmesan cheese

Serves 2

1 Cut off the woody ends from the asparagus. Cut the spears into 2-inch lengths. Bring a small saucepan of water to a boil and cook the asparagus for five minutes until just cooked. Drain and set aside. Reserve the cooking liquid and use to make up the broth.

2 Pour the broth into a saucepan and bring to a boil. Reduce the heat to a gentle simmer.

3 Meanwhile, heat the oil in a large saucepan and gently fry the onion for two minutes until softened, but not browned. Add the rice and cook, stirring, for two minutes.

4 Add a ladleful of broth and cook gently, stirring, until absorbed. Continue ladling in the broth until all the liquid has been absorbed and the rice is thick, creamy, and tender. Keep the heat moderate. This will take about 25 minutes.

5 Stir in the vermouth and cream. Gently mix in the cooked asparagus and season. Serve sprinkled with parmesan.

Dolci

Thanks to Italy's geography and climate, a wide range of delicious fruits is always in season. Fresh fruit is the most popular Italian dessert. However, Italians also lay claim to the invention of icecream, and even the most self-disciplined traveller in Italy will struggle to resist the enticing flavors laid in front of them in every bar-caffè, gelateria, and restaurant. Arguably the best-known dessert in Italy today is tiramisù, literally meaning pick me up—a name derived from the strong shots of coffee it contains.

Honey and pine nut cake

Prep Time:
20 mins

Cooking Time:
1 hour

Sweet, dense, and stickily chewy, this simple cake is fabulous at any time of day.
You could even serve it warm for dessert with whipped cream or ice cream.

～ Ingredients ～

For the cake
2 sticks butter, diced
½ cup clear honey
⅛ cup light corn syrup
½ cup light brown sugar
3 extra-large eggs
⅔ cup toasted pine nuts
2 cups self-rising flour

For the topping
¼ cup toasted pine nuts
4 tbsp. clear honey

Serves 8

1 Preheat the oven to 325°F (160°C). Grease an 8-in. round cake pan and line the bottom with waxed paper.

2 Put the butter, honey, corn syrup, and brown sugar in a saucepan. Heat gently over low heat, stirring, until the butter has melted and the mixture is thoroughly combined. Let cool for about ten minutes. Beat in the eggs, one at a time. Reserve two tablespoons of the pine nuts and stir the rest into the mixture. Sift the flour over the mixture, then stir to combine. Pour the batter into the prepared cake pan. Sprinkle the reserved pine nuts on top.

3 Bake cake for about an hour and ten minutes until a skewer inserted in the center comes out clean. Remove the cake from the oven and let cool in the pan for about five minutes before turning out onto a wire rack.

4 While the cake is warm, prepare the topping. Put the pine nuts and honey in a pan and warm gently until runny. Pour over the cake, spreading the mixture evenly over the top.

Prep Time:
30 mins

Cooking Time:
30 mins

Raspberry genoese

This is the classic whisked sponge cake, and although the method sounds tricky, it's actually very simple. To enjoy it at its best, serve it on the day you make it.

⮌ Ingredients ⮍

3 eggs
⅓ cup superfine sugar
scant ½ cup self-rising flour, sifted
3 tbsp. melted butter
1⅓ cups whipping cream
generous 3 cups fresh raspberries

Serves 8

1 Preheat the oven to 350°F (180°C). Grease two 7-in. round cake pans, and line the bottoms with waxed paper.

2 Put the eggs and sugar in a heat proof bowl over a pan of barely simmering water, making sure the bowl does not touch the water. Whisk for about ten minutes until the mixture is thick and pale and leaves a trail when the whisk is lifted out of the bowl.

3 Sift about three-quarters of the flour over the mixture and fold in. Sift the remaining flour over the mixture and gradually drizzle in the butter as you fold the mixture together. Spoon the batter into the prepared pans and bake for about 30 minutes until risen and golden, and a skewer inserted in the center comes out clean. Turn the cakes out onto a wire rack to cool completely.

4 Just before serving, whip the cream and spread slightly less than half over one cake layer. Sprinkle slightly less than half the raspberries over the whipped cream, then put the second cake layer on top. Top with the remaining whipped cream and raspberries, and serve.

Prep Time:
40 mins

Cooking Time:
60 mins

Rice cake

This traditional dish, *torta di riso*, is a simple but popular northern Italian dessert.

∽ Ingredients ∽

4 cups milk
pinch of salt
2 cups white sugar
zest of 1 lemon
⅛ cup arborio rice
5 egg yolks and 4 egg whites
⅛ cup almonds
⅛ cup pine nuts
⅛ cup candied peel
4 tbsp. grappa
butter, for greasing

Serves 6

1 Preheat the oven. Bring the milk, salt, sugar and lemon to a boil on top of the stove and add the rice.

2 Cook until the rice is completely dissolved. The mixture should have the dense consistency of porridge. Remove it from the heat and let cool.

3 Beat the eggs until well mixed.

4 Lightly toast the almonds and pine nuts. Stir the toasted nuts, candied peel and grappa into the rice mixture, then beat it slowly into the eggs.

5 With the butter, liberally grease a cake pan and pour in the mixture. Bake for about an hour, or until a knife inserted in the center comes out clean. Let the cake cool until it is easy to handle, but still warm, and then ease it from its container.

6 Let stand for as long as possible before serving—this cake will go on improving for up to a week.

Florentines

These rich and sophisticated Italian cookies have always been a favorite.

～ Ingredients ～

6 candied cherries, rinsed and chopped
⅓ cup mixed chopped peel
1 cup roughly chopped mixed nuts
1 tbsp. all-purpose flour
3 tbsp. butter
¼ cup superfine sugar
¼ cup light cream
⅓ cup bittersweet chocolate, broken into squares
1 tsp. coffee extract

1 Preheat the oven to 350°F (180°C). Line two heavy cookie sheets with parchment paper.

2 Mix the fruit and nuts together and chop them finely, then toss them in the flour. Heat the butter, sugar, and cream together until the butter has melted, then bring just to a boil. Add the prepared fruits, and stir well.

3 Put spoonfuls of mixture on the cookie sheets, allowing room for them to spread. Bake for 15 to 20 minutes, until golden. Cool slightly, then transfer to a wire rack to cool.

4 Melt the chocolate in a bowl over a saucepan of simmering water. Stir in the coffee extract. Spread a little of the chocolate thinly over the back of each florentine, then leave them face down on the wire rack to set.

Makes about 16

Prep Time:
20 mins

Cooking Time:
30 mins

Panforte

This spicy recipe comes from Tuscany. It dates back to the thirteenth century, when it was known as *panpepato*, and was paid to the monks and nuns of a monastery as tax each year.

～ Ingredients ～

3½ oz. shelled almonds
3½ oz. hazelnuts
3½ oz. shelled walnuts
5oz. dried figs
5oz. mixed candied fruit
5oz. confectioners' sugar
3½ oz. honey
¼ tsp. cinnamon
a good pinch of ground cloves
¼ tsp. ground coriander
½ tsp. ground ginger
a good pinch of nutmeg
approx. 2 tbsp. flour
butter for greasing the tins
confectioners' sugar for dusting

1 Preheat oven to (300°F/150°C). Toast the nuts briefly in a skillet. Let cool then, chop them roughly.

2 Finely dice the candied fruit and figs, put into a bowl, add the spices and nuts, and mix.

3 Put the confectioners' sugar and honey into a metal bowl and put over a bain-marie. Stir constantly over a low heat until the mixture melts and forms threads. Let cool slightly, stirring constantly.

4 Stir the honey mixture into the prepared fruit and nuts and mix in two tbsp. flour. Line the compartments of two muffin tins with parchment paper, turn the mixture into them and smooth the top.

5 Bake in the oven for 25–30 minutes. Take out and let cool. Dust with confectioners' sugar.

Makes 20 portions

Prep Time:
30 mins

Cooking Time:
1 hour

Sweet ricotta tart

Variations of this tart are prepared all over Italy in celebration of Easter.

∽ Ingredients ∽

1¾ cups all-purpose flour

½ cup confectioners' sugar

½ tsp. salt

½ tsp. baking powder

zest of 1 lemon

½ cup unsalted butter, cut into small pieces

2 large eggs, lightly beaten

2 cups ricotta

⅓ cup cream cheese, softened

1 tbsp. cornstarch

1 tsp. vanilla extract

2 large eggs, lightly beaten

½ cup superfine sugar

zest of 1 lemon

Makes 20 portions

1 Preheat the oven to 350°F (180°C).

2 To make the piecrust, combine the flour, sugar, salt, baking powder, and lemon zest in a large bowl. Cut the butter into the flour mixture, until the mixture resembles coarse meal. Add the eggs and stir until the mixture begins to form large clumps.

3 Turn out onto a lightly floured surface and knead until the pastry is smooth, about one minute. Divide the pastry into two discs, one slightly larger. Wrap the smaller disc in plastic wrap and refrigerate. Press the larger disc around the base and up the sides of a 9-in. tart pan. To make the filling, put the cheeses, cornstarch, and vanilla in a large bowl. Using an electric mixer, beat on medium speed until smooth. Add the eggs, sugar, and lemon zest. Beat until well combined.

4 Spoon the filling into the tart shell, and smooth the top with a spatula. Remove the smaller pastry disc from the refrigerator. Put on a lightly floured surface and roll out to a 10-in. round. Put the round over the cheese filling, trim the excess from the edges, and make four slits in the top. Bake in the middle of the oven for an hour, or until the pastry has puffed up and is golden brown.

Biscotti

Prep Time:
20 mins

Cooking Time:
60 mins

These twice-baked Italian biscuits can be enjoyed with coffee or served with sorbet as a dessert.

～ Ingredients ～

2 cups all-purpose flour
1 cup superfine sugar
1 tsp. baking powder
¼ tsp. salt
3 eggs
2 tsp. vanilla extract
1 cup whole blanched almonds

Makes 40

1 Preheat the oven to 300°F (150°C). Grease and flour two baking sheets. Mix the dry ingredients together in a large bowl. Whisk the eggs and vanilla extract together then stir into the dry ingredients. Add the almonds and stir them into the dough. The dough should be sticky.

2 Divide the dough between the baking sheets and shape into two flat loaves about ten inches long and two inches wide. Bake for 35–40 minutes until pale golden. Remove from the oven on to a chopping board and immediately slice into thin pieces about ½ in. wide.

3 Lay the slices back onto the baking sheets and cook for 10–15 minutes. Turn over each slice and cook for a further ten to 15 minutes, or until the slices are golden brown. Remove from the oven and let cool.

4 When cool, store in an airtight container. The biscotti will keep for a couple of weeks.

Panettone

Prep Time:
45 mins

Cooking Time:
50 mins

Usually prepared and enjoyed around Christmastime in Italy, this sweet bread is one of the culinary symbols of Milan.

∽ Ingredients ∽

2 x 25 oz. panettone tins
(or Kugelhopf tins)
3½ oz. raisins
1½ oz. candied orange peel
1½ oz. candied lemon peel
2 tbsp. rum
1½ oz. pine nuts

For the dough:
½ cube yeast or 1 tsp. active dry yeast
7 fl. oz. lukewarm milk
2 cups flour
1¾ oz. sugar
1 tsp. vanilla extract
a good pinch of salt
2 egg yolks
3½ oz. soft butter
1 tsp. each of grated orange and lemon peel
a good pinch of ground aniseed
fat to grease the tins
butter for brushing

1 Preheat oven to 320°F (160°C). Finely chop the candied peel and soak in the rum with the raisins.

2 Put all the dough ingredients into a bowl, mix and knead well. Cover with a cloth and put in a warm, draught-free place to rise, until it has doubled in volume.

3 Knead the soaked fruit, candied peel, and pine nuts into the dough and divide the dough into two portions.

4 Put into the well-greased tins and leave to rise for a further 20 minutes or so.

5 Put risen dough into preheated oven, two shelves from the bottom, and bake at for 50–60 minutes.

6 After 15–20 minutes brush the surface of the panettone with a little butter and bake until done. Turn out of the tins and cool on a cake rack.

Serves 8

Prep Time:
20 mins

Cooking Time:
0 mins

Zabaglione

This delicious, creamy Italian dessert is whipped into a lovely light treat.

∽ Ingredients ∾

6 eggs
¾ cup confectioners' sugar
6 tbsp. Marsala

Serves 6

1 Separate the eggs. Beat the yolks, mixing in with the sugar and Marsala. Transfer the bowl containing the egg mixture into the saucepan filled with hot water, or pour into the egg mixture into the top part of a double boiler.

2 Begin to beat the egg mixture with a balloon whisk or a hand-held electric mixer. As the air is incorporated into the eggs, it will swell from the heat of the water, becoming firmer as it cooks.

3 Whisk until the mixture increases its volume by at least 3 times and stiffens until it is only just pourable.

4 Pour into glasses and serve with Italian biscuits.

Tiramisù

Tiramisù

Prep Time:
30 mins
Chilling Time:
20 mins

∾ Ingredients ∾

4 eggs

4 tbsp. Marsala

4 oz. confectioners' sugar

4 oz. mascarpone

1 cup strong coffee, sweetened with

2 oz. white sugar

40 ladyfinger biscuits

4 oz. bittersweet chocolate

Serves 8

1 Separate the eggs. In a small bowl, combine the yolks, Marsala, and sugar and beat together. Bring a pan of water to just below boiling point, then turn down to a simmer and beat the yolk mixture over the water until it begins to swell and thicken. Use a double boiler, if you have one. Set the yolks aside.

2 Whisk two of the whites into stiff peaks and fold them into the yolk mixture, then set aside.

3 Liquidize the mascarpone in a food processor or blender and fold into it the yolk and white mixture. Check the sweetness at this stage and adjust it to taste.

4 Dip each biscuit in the coffee; let them soak well. Arrange a floor of biscuits on a dish, then spread them with a thin coating of the egg-mascarpone mixture. Repeat the process until you have used your last layer. Run a knife around the edges of the dish to smooth down the sides. Grate the chocolate and sprinkle it over sides and top. Chill until completely cold and set.

Fig and ricotta tarts

Prep Time:
15 mins

Cooking Time:
10 mins

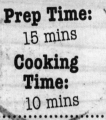

Fresh figs have long been accompanied by ricotta and honey; here this combination is lovingly assembled in tartlet shells.

∽ Ingredients ∼

For the crust:
2 cups all-purpose flour
⅛ tsp. salt
½ cup vegetable shortening
½ cup cold unsalted butter
1 large egg
2 tsp. white vinegar
2 tbsp. ice-cold water

For the filling:
⅔ cup ricotta, drained
⅓ cup sour cream
2 tbsp. confectioners' sugar
1 tsp. vanilla extract
8–10 fresh figs, sliced in rounds
¼ cup honey

Makes 12–18

1 Preheat the oven to 375°F (190°C). Combine the flour and salt in a large mixing bowl. Cut the vegetable shortening and butter into small chunks and add to the flour mixture. Using a pastry blender or two knives in a criss-crossing motion, blend the butter and shortening into the flour mixture until it has the consistency of damp sand, with a few pea-sized pieces of butter and shortening remaining. Using a fork or wire whisk, beat the egg with the vinegar and water. Slowly pour the egg mixture over the flour, stirring only until the mixture is moist. Divide the dough into two balls and wrap each one in plastic wrap. Chill in the refrigerator for a minimum of half an hour.

2 On a lightly floured surface, remove from the wrap and roll out half the quantity of the pastry dough. Using a 3-in. round cutter, cut out circles of pastry. Gently push the circles into the cups of a 12-cup muffin pan. Collect the scraps, roll out, and repeat. Roll out the second disc of pastry dough. Each disc should yield 9 tartlet shells, but if you prefer a thick crust, make fewer (six per disc). Bake for 8–10 minutes.

3 To make the filling, combine the ricotta, cream, confectioners' sugar, and vanilla. Whisk until smooth. Fill each tartlet shell with the ricotta mixture and arrange two or three fig rounds, overlapping, over the filling. Warm the honey in a small saucepan over low heat. Using a pastry brush, glaze each tart. Serve chilled.

Prep Time:
20 mins

Chilling Time:
15 mins

Gelato di 'crema

This simplest of Italian ice creams is made with a cooked egg custard and cream and can be used as the basis for almost all other gelato flavors. It is also delicious just on its own.

∽ Ingredients ∽

2½ cups light cream
5 egg yolks
½ cup superfine sugar

Makes about 4 cups

1 Heat the cream until it is beginning to bubble, then let cool slightly.

2 In a large heatproof bowl, beat the egg yolks and sugar until thick and creamy. Beat the cooling cream gently into the eggs.

3 Put the bowl over a pan of gently simmering water and stir with a wooden spoon until the custard just coats the back of the spoon. Remove the bowl and let cool.

4 When the custard is completely cooled, pour into an ice cream maker and process according to the manufacturer's directions. Stop churning when it is almost firm, transfer to a freezer container, and leave in the freezer for 15 minutes before serving, or until required.

5 This gelato is best eaten fresh, but it can be frozen for up to a month. Take out at least 15 minutes before serving to soften slightly.

Apple, pear, and cinnamon risotto

Prep Time: 15 mins

Cooking Time: 25 mins

This is a real orchard risotto, delicately flavored with cinnamon to bring out the best in the fruits.

～ Ingredients ～

2 pints apple juice

2 oz. butter

2 tsp. ground cinnamon

1 oz. brown sugar

14 oz. arborio rice

2 red dessert apples, cored and sliced

2 dessert pears, cored and sliced

1 oz. pecan halves

Serves 4

1 Pour the apple juice into a saucepan and bring to a boil. Reduce the heat to a gentle simmer.

2 Meanwhile, melt half of the butter in a large skillet and add the cinnamon, sugar, and rice. Cook gently, stirring constantly, for two minutes until the rice is well coated in butter.

3 Add a ladleful of apple juice and cook gently, stirring all the time, until absorbed. Continue adding apple juice in small quantities until the risotto is thick but not sticky, about 25 minutes.

4 Meanwhile, melt the remaining butter in a separate skillet and cook the apples, pears, and pecans for three to four minutes, stirring. Add the contents of the pan to the rice, mix gently, and serve.

Tutti-frutti gelato

Tutti-frutti gelato

Add a riot of colors and flavors to a simple gelato and create your own masterpiece.

∾ Ingredients ∾

1 recipe gelato di crema (page 180)
1 cup chopped crystallized
or candied fruits
(cherries, pineapple, citrus peel, ginger)

1 Prepare the basic gelato (page 180) and churn until partly frozen. Mix in your preferred fruits and freeze until required.

2 Although best eaten fresh, this gelato can be frozen for up to a month. Take out of the freezer 15 minutes before serving to soften slightly.

Makes about 4 cups

Lemon and mint gelato

Lemon and mint gelato

Prep Time:
20 mins

Cooking Time:
15 mins

This is a delicately lemon-flavored gelato, perfect to enjoy with fresh fruits.

∽ Ingredients ∽

1 recipe gelato di crema
2 unwaxed lemons
1 tbsp. chopped fresh mint leaves

Makes about 4 cups

1 Prepare the basic gelato di crema (page 180) and then blend in the finely grated zest of the lemons, the mint leaves, and the juice of the lemons.

2 Pour into an ice cream maker and process according to the manufacturer's instructions. Stop churning when it is almost firm, transfer to a freezer container, and leave in the freezer for 15 minutes before serving, or until required.

3 This gelato is best eaten fresh, but it can be frozen for up to a month. Take out of the freezer 15 minutes before serving to soften slightly.

Sunshine fruit risotto

186

sunshine fruit risotto

This is a really colorful risotto, with the different fruits complementing each other in tone and flavor.

~ Ingredients ~

3 cups pineapple juice

4 tbsp. butter

2¼ tbsp. soft brown sugar

2 cups arborio rice

1 tsp. ground cinnamon

1 tsp. ground allspice

8 oz. fresh pineapple, peeled, cored, and cubed

1 papaya, halved, seeded, and sliced

1 mango, peeled and sliced

1 Pour the pineapple juice into a saucepan and bring to a boil. Reduce the heat to a gentle simmer.

2 Meanwhile, melt the butter in a large skillet and stir in the sugar and rice. Add the spices and cook gently, stirring constantly, until the rice is well coated in butter.

3 Add a ladleful of pineapple juice and cook gently, stirring, until absorbed. Continue adding pineapple juice in small quantities for 20 minutes. Stir in the fruit and cook for a further five minutes until the risotto is thick but not sticky. Serve in a warm dish.

Serves 4

Strawberry gelato

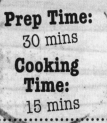

Prep Time:
30 mins

Cooking Time:
15 mins

strawberry gelato

When made with really sweet, ripe strawberries, this gelato is sure to bring back happy memories of childhood. Enjoy it simply on its own.

∽ Ingredients ∾

1 recipe gelato di crema (page 180)
3½ cups hulled and chopped fresh strawberries
2 tbsp. superfine sugar
1 tsp. lemon juice
1 tsp. pure vanilla extract

Makes about 4 cups

1 Prepare the basic gelato recipe (page 180) and let cool completely.

2 Purée the strawberries in a blender or food processor with the sugar, lemon juice, and vanilla extract. Pour through a fine-mesh strainer to remove seeds, if desired.

3 Stir the strawberry purée into the basic gelato until well blended. Pour into an ice cream maker and process according to the manufacturer's directions. Stop churning when it is almost firm, transfer to a freezer container, and leave in the freezer for 15 minutes before serving, or until required.

4 This gelato is best eaten within a month. Take out 15 minutes before serving to soften.

Index

Credits

A = above, B = below
Shutterstock images appear on pages: 2, 5, 6, 7, 8, 9, 11, 13B, 15, 34, 36, 45, 49, 52, 56, 59, 69, 72, 88, 91, 93, 105B, 110, 137, 148, 151, 157, 176, 186
StockFood images appear on pages: 30, 46, 61, 62, 64, 67, 71, 96, 101, 102, 107, 108, 113, 118, 120, 123, 125, 126, 130, 133, 134, 143, 144, 148, 152, 155, 162, 164, 166, 172, 174
Jupiter images appear on page: 11B
Getty images appear of page: 13A, 105A

All other images are the copyright of Quintet Publishing Ltd. While every effort has been made to credit contributors, Quintet Publishing would like to apologize should there have been any omissions or errors— and would be pleased to make the appropriate correction for future editions of the book.